SEALINK BRITISH FERRIES

Ian Collard

AMBERLEY

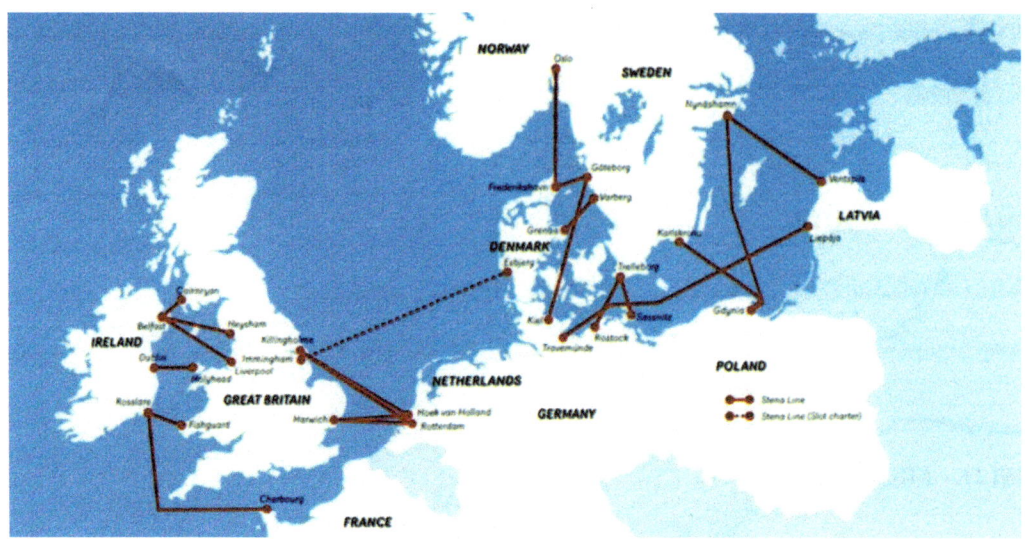

First published 2019

Amberley Publishing
The Hill, Stroud, Gloucestershire, GL5 4EP
www.amberley-books.com

Copyright © Ian Collard, 2019

The right of Ian Collard to be identified as the Author of this work has been asserted in accordance with the Copyrights, Designs and Patents Act 1988.

ISBN 978 1 4456 9304 0 (print)
ISBN 978 1 4456 9305 7 (ebook)

All rights reserved. No part of this book may be reprinted or reproduced or utilised in any form or by any electronic, mechanical or other means, now known or hereafter invented, including photocopying and recording, or in any information storage or retrieval system, without the permission in writing from the Publishers.

British Library Cataloguing in Publication Data.
A catalogue record for this book is available from the British Library.

Origination by Amberley Publishing.
Printed in Great Britain.

Introduction

The London, Midland & Scottish Railway had the largest railway-owned fleet in the world and was the only railway company to maintain cross-Channel or short sea routes on both sides of Britain. It was also the only company to maintain regular passenger services on a lake in England. The route from Holyhead to Dun Laoghaire was the first short sea service to be operated by a railway company, and dates back to 1848. Cargo and livestock services were also maintained between Holyhead and Dublin and Holyhead and Greenore.

The east coast services were operated by the Associated Humber Lines, who maintained a passenger and cargo service from Goole and Hull to Amsterdam, Antwerp, Copenhagen, Ghent, Hamburg and Rotterdam. The service to Ulster offered an alternative route to that provided by the Belfast Steamship Company from Liverpool. The Tilbury–Gravesend ferry was also operated by the company and the two main steamers on Lake Windermere, *Teal* and *Swan*, were introduced in 1936 and 1938 respectively. The passenger services on the Clyde gave connections from St Enoch, Glasgow, to the Clyde resorts via Greenock (Princes Pier), Gourock, Ardrossan, Fairlie and Ayr. The London, Midland & Scottish Railway also maintained a joint service with the London & North Eastern Railway on Loch Lomond. It was claimed that by using the 'express business man's service' on the Stranraer–Larne route one could leave Belfast on the 6.25 p.m. sailing and be in your office in London at 9 o'clock the following morning.

The fleet of the London, Midland & Scottish Railway included cross-channel ships of passenger and mail type, cross-channel ships carrying cargo and cattle, short sea vessels of North Sea type, fast turbine-driven excursion vessels, paddle ships, lake vessels, dredgers, tugs, lighters and some other craft. The Great Western Railway operated from Rosslare and Waterford and from Weymouth to the Channel Islands, Guernsey and Jersey. The Fishguard to Rosslare route provided a passenger and cargo service and the Fishguard to Waterford a passenger, cargo and cattle service. A fleet of tenders for passenger liners was also operated by the company at Plymouth and during the summer months cruises and excursions were offered from Weymouth, Plymouth, Torquay and the Channel Islands by these small vessels.

In 1934 the extension of Parkeston Quay, known as Parkeston Quay West, was opened. It was equipped with a maritime station, transit sheds and cranes. It extended the old quay by 1,120 feet and provided berths for three vessels, making the total length of quay space at Parkeston over 4,000 feet. The quay was used by passengers arriving from Liverpool Street station, the Midlands and the North, with through coaches to and from Birmingham, Coventry, Doncaster, Manchester, Sheffield, Liverpool and Warrington. For many years, if judged by the number of foreign visitors arriving and departing from the United Kingdom, Harwich ranked as the second busiest port in Britain.

The main route from Parkeston Quay was the service to the Hook of Holland. At the Dutch port passengers had the choice of the North German Express to Berlin with a through coach to Hamburg and connections to Hanover to Leipzig, Dresden and Prague, the Rheingold Express along the Rhine Valley to Switzerland and the Balkan Express, with through coaches to Vienna and Budapest and connections to Bucharest. There was also a nightly service from Parkeston Quay to Antwerp, with a boat train connection to Brussels. As a full English breakfast was served on the outward journey and a table d'hôte dinner homeward, the vessels on this route were provided with considerable galley and restaurant facilities. The United Steamship Company provided a daily service to Esbjerg and the Zeeland Steamship Company offered a passenger and cargo route to Flushing. During the summer season passengers were able to sail to Zeebrugge.

Belgian Railways & Marine operated the Ostend–Dover service. The mail service between Ostend and Dover was inaugurated on 8 April 1815, and was only operated by ships flying the British flag up to 1846. There were four sailings a week in each direction, and the crossing took from five to seven hours. When the railway lines were opened between Ostend and Brussels in 1838 and between Dover and London in

1841 the Belgian Government built a fleet of steamships to be employed on the route. By 1848 the Belgian ships were making eight crossings and the British ships six, which made a total of fourteen crossings a week. From 1862 the service was operated by the Belgian Government alone and the following year they had seven ships operating two services each day.

By 1892 the Belgian fleet consisted of nine ships with first class saloons aft, a large promenade deck and a number of single cabins. Ordered in 1905, the *Princesse Elisabeth* achieved 24 knots on trials, becoming the fastest ship of her class in the world. During the First World War all of the ships were used for the evacuation of Belgian refugees and crossed the Channel more than 4,000 times, carrying over 2 million soldiers and 500,000 wounded. In 1936 Belgian Marine converted the *Ville de Liege* to a car ferry. She was able to carry eighty cars on covered decks and 265 passengers. She was able to embark and disembark cars without the aid of cranes, by means of mobile ramps, whatever the state of the tide and without using a special dock.

The ports of Dover and Harwich differed from all other cross-Channel ports in the country in that they incorporated facilities for railway wagons and carriages to be shipped on specially designed train ferries. This facility eliminated the need to unload onto quays, cranage and other stevedoring activities. A truck loaded anywhere in Britain could be sent to any station in Europe outside Spain and Russia, where the railway gauges were different. The train ferries operated from Dover to Dunkirk and Harwich to Zeebrugge. Handling of the cargo was reduced to a minimum, the risk of damage or loss was slight and insurance rates were lower for goods transported in this manner. It was the quickest, safest and easiest way of moving goods across the Continent. The rolling stock included covered and open, refrigerated and insulated wagons, and also motor car trucks. Private owners' tank wagons were also conveyed.

A new dock was built at Dover in which the ship was shut off from the sea by double gates. The water level inside the dock was lowered or raised by pumps, and the rails on the ship were connected with the rails ashore by a link-span. The connection between ship and shore at Harwich was by means of an adjustable bridge secured at the shore end by resting on the ship. The length of this bridge was governed by the rise and fall of the tide, so that at either high or low water the safe working gradient did not exceed 1 in 20. The Harwich–Zeebrugge service was under the management of the London & North Eastern Railway, which owned the ships and the terminal installation at Harwich. The terminal at Zeebrugge was owned and operated by the Société Belgo-Anglaise des Ferryboats. The Dover–Dunkirk service was managed by the Southern Railway in conjunction with the AIA Steamship Company, which was responsible for all the arrangements at Dunkirk. The train ferry service operated from Victoria station to Dover and across the Channel to Dunkirk and then to Paris. Twelve luxurious sleeping cars were built especially for this service and ticket inspections took place after eight o'clock in the morning, as the train was arriving at Paris. The train ferries also carried twenty-five cars in a large garage above the train deck.

The Southern Railway operated from Dover to Calais, Folkestone to Boulogne, Newhaven to Dieppe and Dover to Ostend with Belgian Railways. Dover–Calais was the link for the Golden Arrow, the Brussels Pullman, the Blue Train and Simplon Orient Express, the Orient Express, the Rome Express, the Engadine Express and the Bombay Express. One of the main steamers on the route was the *Canterbury*, which was described in Southern Railway brochures as follows:

> You will discover the harmony between these trains and the ship. The awning deck is enclosed by glass windows, making it both sheltered and light. Instead of ordinary deck chairs, there are armchairs upholstered in velvet. In addition to a large number of cabins, there are screened off alcoves. The ships also have a spacious dining saloon with accommodation for 100 people and a comfortable lounge, a buffet and a bar. The whole of the interior is of carefully selected wood, panelled and suitably decorated.

In 1938 over 50,000 people travelled by the Calais route in a summer month, and the previous year over 111,000 people passed through Folkestone, of which 32,000 were on excursions to France. The Newhaven–Dieppe route was operated by six ships and jointly owned by the French State Railways and the Southern Railway. This service route was operated to fulfil two functions. The first was to take people to the strip of coast that includes Pourville and Le Tréport, and the second was to provide a cheap route to Paris. Passenger traffic to Belgium increased steadily during the 1930s and all records were broken in 1937, when the total number of passengers that travelled by the Dover–Ostend route was 778,961. This was an increase of 110,000 over the previous year.

The Southampton–Havre service was operated by the London and South Western Railway and was popular with travellers to France from the Midlands and the West and North of England, as it avoided London. It was also a perfect starting point for the arrival of thousands of visitors by ocean liners travelling to mainland Europe. The services to Jersey and Guernsey were operated jointly with Southern Railway steamers, sailing on alternative days with the Great Western Railway via Weymouth in winter months. In the summer, the Southern Railway steamers sailed from Southampton.

The Transport Bill was introduced on 28 November 1946 'to bring transport services, essential to the well-being of the nation under public ownership and control'. The Act covered fifty-nine rail-oriented bodies and was passed in Parliament on 6 August 1947, creating the British Transport Commission. Shareholders were paid compensation in 3 per cent stock in exchange for railway stock fixed on prices between February and June 1945 or November 1946, whichever was most advantageous.

On 1 January 1948 the four major railway companies – the London, Midland & Scottish, London & North Eastern Railway, Southern Railway and the Great Western Railway – were nationalised, becoming part of the British Transport Commission (British Railways). The companies were redesignated as Regions, with the addition of the Scottish Region, which comprised the former LNER and LMS north of the border. They were originally controlled by six railway executives with the English operations of the LNER being divided into two Regions. The railway executives were later reduced to five when the Eastern and North Eastern Regions were combined. The French-owned SNCF operated alongside the ships of the Southern Region on the Dover and Newhaven routes and the Zeeland Shipping Company with the Eastern Region ships on the Harwich–Hook of Holland service. The Belgium Marine Administration provided services on the Ostend–Dover service and the Caledonian Steam Packet Company continued to manage the fleet of Clyde steamers.

Maid of Orleans entered service on 23 June 1949, and she was followed by *Brighton* the following year. *Brighton* worked with the French vessels *Londres* and *Arromanches* and the *Lisieux*. The *Lisieux* was one of the fastest Channel vessels, with a speed of 25.4 knots on her trials. *Cote d'Azur* was introduced in 1950 and *Normannia* followed two years later. *Normannia* was allocated to the Le Havre route but did relieve on the Harwich–Hook of Holland service when required. *Normannia* and *Falaise* were later converted to roll-on/roll-off car ferries for the Dover–Calais route. *Prince Phillippe* and *Koning Albert* were introduced by the Belgium Marine Administration following the loss of the *Princes Astrid* in 1949, off Dunkirk. *Princes Josephine Charlotte* was retired and her name transferred to a new vessel in 1949. *Amsterdam* and *Arnhem* operated on the Harwich–Hook of Holland service and *Cambria* and *Hibernia* entered service on the Holyhead–Dun Laoghaire route in 1949.

Lord Warden, the first purpose-built British car ferry, entered service between Dover and Boulogne in 1952 and was designed to carry 120 cars. She used the newly opened car ferry berth at the Gare Maritime at Boulogne. However, cars had to be craned on and off at Dover until the car ferry berth was opened at the Eastern Docks in June 1953. The new terminal incorporated vehicle marshalling areas, customs inspection sheds and a terminal building with shopping, lounge and restaurant areas.

On 6 May 1953 the *Duke of York* collided with the *Haiti Victory* in the Channel and during repairs she was rebuilt and modernised before being returned to the Harwich service. The Belgium Marine Administration introduced the new *Rio Leopold III*, *Koningin Elizabeth* and the *Reine Astrid*. The three vessels were built by Cockerill Ougree. In 1955 it was reported that the railways were operating in deficit and it was felt that a degree of restructuring was required to enable them to operate on an economic basis.

The London Midland Region of British Railways ordered three vessels which took their names from the previous ships on the Heysham–Belfast route. *Duke of Lancaster* and *Duke of Argyll* entered service in 1956, followed by *Duke of Rothesay* the following year. *Artevelde* was introduced in 1958, becoming the first Belgian ferry to be fitted with stabilisers. The French National Railway's first car ferry, *Compiegne*, also came into service in 1958 and was able to carry 164 cars and 1,000 passengers. *Maid of Kent* was introduced the following year and the French car ferry *Chantilly* in 1960.

Caesarea and *Sarnia* replaced *St Helier* and *St Julien* on the service from Weymouth to the Channel Islands in 1960–61. The Southampton–Channel Islands route was closed and *Isle of Guernsey* was retained in service until 1969. The Zeeland Steam Ship Company introduced the *Koningin Wilhelmina* on the Harwich–Hook service on 7 February 1960 and British Rail's *Avalon* became the last conventional vessel to be ordered by the British Transport Commission. She sailed on her maiden voyage on 25 July 1963, replacing the *Duke of York*. *Avalon* was later converted to provide cruises to Scandinavia and the Northern capitals, Oporto, Lisbon and Gibraltar.

In June 1961 Dr Beeching was appointed on a five-year secondment from Imperial Chemical Industries to become Chairman of the British Transport Commission and the British Railways Board. The British Transport Commission included British Road Services, Hotels and Catering, Thomas Tilling, Thos Cook & Son, Pullman Car Company, Atlantic Transport Line and several other smaller organisations. On 1 January 1963 the British Railways Board was formed and all rail services owned by the British Transport Commission were formed into separate Holdings Organisations. Tugs and dredgers were no longer railway owned and were transferred to the British Transport Docks Board. The British Waterways Board took over all canals and navigable rivers. Dr Beeching's report *The Reshaping of British Railways* was published on 25 March 1963 and it recommended that 17,500 miles of route (34,150 miles of track) would be reduced to 11,000 miles and steam phased out by 1968. In November 1965 the first of five Freightliner routes was introduced with permanently coupled, newly designed rolling stock for the carriage of containers.

In the early 1960s the popularity of the Dover–Ostend route was increasing and *Koningin Fabiola* entered service in 1962, followed by *Roi Baudouin* in 1965 and *Princes Astrid* three years later. British Railways announced the closure of all passenger services from Southampton after 1963 and *Normannia* and *Falaise* were withdrawn and converted into stern-loading car ferries. *Falaise* was moved to Newhaven and *Normannia* to the Dover–Boulogne route. With the increase in traffic on the Newhaven–Dieppe route it was decided to build a new car ferry terminal at Newhaven and *Villandry* and *Valencay* were ordered for this service.

The car ferry *Dover* came into service in 1965 and the Terminal at Dover was enlarged to cater for the increased ferry traffic at the port. Belgium Marine's last conventional passenger vessel, *Prinses Paola* was launched on 12 February 1966 and made her inaugural voyage to Dover on 14 June that year. She was nicknamed locally in Dover as the 'Racing Greyhound'. The name Sealink was adopted for marketing purposes and the ships' hulls were painted in a blue colour scheme, with a logo of opposed arrows in white on a red background on red funnels. The vessels were painted in the new colours from early in 1965 with the name Sealink on the ships' hulls. The Eastern and North Eastern Regions were amalgamated on 1 January 1967 and the following year the Shipping & International Services Division was formed as well as the Scottish Transport Group, to take over the Caledonian and MacBrayne ships, and to link them with the local transport services. *Antrim Princess* and *St George* were delivered in 1967 and 1968 respectively, with *Ailsa Princess* joining the fleet in 1971.

The hovercraft division of British Railways introduced the Mountbatten Class SRN4 *The Princess Margaret* in 1968. She carried 250 passengers and thirty cars between the Eastern Docks at Dover and Le Portel, near Boulogne. *The Princess Anne* was also introduced on this service and both craft were later lengthened to increase their capacity to 400 passengers and fifty-four cars. A new hoverport was built in 1978, next to the Prince of Wales Pier at Dover. The Belgian Marine Administration decided to provide a high-speed service by the Boeing Jetfoils *Princesse Clementine* and *Prinses Stephanie* in 1981. The *Reine Astrid*, which had been withdrawn in 1981, was permanently berthed at the Admiralty Pier to provide check-in and other facilities for the jetfoil service. The hovercraft operations of Hoverlloyd and Seaspeed were amalgamated and merged as Hoverspeed in 1981, with services concentrated at Dover. The company changed hands with a management buyout in 1984 and was taken over by Sea Containers two years later. The Seacat's *Hoverspeed Great Britain* and *Hoverspeed France* were introduced on the service from Dover to Calais and Boulogne in 1991, with *Hoverspeed Boulogne* operating from Folkestone to Boulogne following the closure of the conventional car ferry service the following year.

In 1970 the marketing name Sealink was adopted and in November that year Belgium Marine joined the Sealink consortium, becoming the Belgian Maritime Transport Authority – Regie voor Maritiem Transport Authority (RMT) – on 1 November 1971. The Zeeland Shipping Company and SNCF also assumed the Sealink identity. It was announced that the facilities at the port of Folkestone would receive a substantial investment and the port would be modernised and upgraded to provide purpose-built facilities for passengers and cars. A new passenger terminal was constructed next to Folkestone Harbour station and a vehicle loading ramp was built. The *Hengist* and *Horsa* were introduced in 1972 for the service between Folkestone and Boulogne. They were the first ships in the fleet to have the name Sealink painted along their sides. *Senlac* was built to operate on the Newhaven–Dieppe service in 1973 to replace the *Falaise*, which was transferred to Weymouth. *Svea Drott* was purchased for this route, renamed *Earl Godwin*, and *Maid of Kent* was placed on a new Sealink service from Weymouth to Cherbourg. The Belgian vessels *Prins Philippe* and *Prince Laurent* were introduced on the Dover–Ostend route as the first Belgium drive-through vessels. A new car ferry berth was opened at the Admiralty Pier at Dover in 1974, to provide sailings to Calais and Ostend, with boat train connections for foot passengers. *St Edmund* was delivered for the Harwich–Hook of Holland route in 1974 and the *St Columba* for the Holyhead–Dun Laoghaire service the following year. *Chartres* was delivered to SNCF, and *Prinses Maria Esmeralda* and *Princesse Marie Christine* also came into service on the Channel in 1974 and 1975, followed by the *Prins Albert* in 1978. *Prinses Beatrix* was delivered to the Zeeland Shipping Company in 1978, becoming the largest vessel to operate under the Sealink banner at that time.

Sealink UK Limited was formed on 1 January 1979, with the subsidiaries ALA, Sealink, Isle of Man (Manx Line Holdings Limited), Fishguard & Rosslare Dock & Harbour Company Limited, Passtruck (Shipping) Company Limited, Passro (Shipping) Company Limited and Sealink (Scotland) Limited. The company was based at Eversholt House, London, and the shipping was divided into divisions: Continental and Channel Islands, Irish, Isle of Wight, Isle of Man and Esturial and the ports of Dover, Fishguard, Folkestone, Heysham, Holyhead, Newhaven, Parkeston Quay, Portsmouth, Stranraer and Weymouth. The ship's hull colour reverted from blue to black. The following year the pooling arrangement with Townsend Thoresen ended. *Galloway Princess* entered service in April 1980, followed by *St Anselm*, *St Christopher*, *St David* and *Cote d'Azur* was delivered in 1981.

On 14 July 1980 it was announced by the Transport Minister that the shipping, hovercraft and hotels sections of British Rail would be denationalised within two or three years. The Virgin Island-based Sea Containers purchased the company on 27 July 1984 for the sum of £66 million. It was described as 'the sale of the century'. Sea Containers acquired thirty-seven ships, ten harbours and twenty-four established routes. The new owners quickly renamed the company Sealink British Ferries, with a livery which comprised a dark blue funnel, with stylised officer's ranking stripes in gold and white hull with Sealink on the sides in blue letters, followed by British Ferries. *Champs Elysees* was delivered in 1984 and *Koningin Beatrix* to the Zeeland Shipping Company two years later.

In February 1985 the trading name of the company was altered to Sealink British Ferries, who then entered an agreement with the British & Irish Steam Packet Company to rationalise sailings in the Irish Sea. This arrangement attempted to provide for cooperation between the two companies but did not survive due to major financial problems experienced by the British & Irish Steam Packet. The relationship between the two companies was further strained in April 1987 when Sealink introduced the freight ship *Stena Sailer* to supplement sailings, instead of using a British and Irish vessel. Consequently, at the end of that year the Irish company withdrew from the pooling agreement with Sealink.

Fiesta and *Fantasia* entered service in 1990 on the Channel routes. Named *Scandinavia*, *Fantasia* had begun her operational life in 1980 as one of three 'Challenger' class roll-on/roll-off vessels for the Swedish company Rederi AB Nordo. Together with her sister *Ariadne*, the ships were built taking advantage of the Swedish Government's aid on offer for ships ordered domestically by Swedish shipowners. They were designed for routes from Greece to Syria as part of the Greece–Syria Express Line, although they actually operated initially for UMEF from Yugoslavia to Tartous in Syria. The vessels were constructed to a particularly high specification, with accommodation for over 100 drivers and featuring large twin freight decks, and were of a notably innovative design. In October 1988 the two ships passed to Sealink as part of a deal, the Bulgarians receiving in part exchange the *Seafreight Freeway* and *Seafreight Highway*. A conversion contract was awarded to Lloyd Werft at Bremerhaven, with *Fiesta* entering dry dock in June 1989. During the conversion it was decided that the ships should swap names, *Fantasia* becoming the lead ship, with the name *Fiesta* being given to the second vessel. The conversion included the fitting of large side sponsons to aid stability and the main passenger deck was largely fitted into the original superstructure. The excess height of the two original freight decks, which were designed to carry stacked containers, was reduced by lowering the height of the upper deck, and the new passenger level fitted above in the space saved. Capacity for 1,800 passengers and 723 cars was specified.

In 1990, following a lengthy battle, Sealink British Ferries was acquired by the Swedish Stena Line for £259 million. They purchased all of Sea Containers' English Channel, Irish Sea and North Sea ships and services. Sea Containers retained the cross-Channel hovercraft services, its Isle of Wight services, its share in the Isle of Man Steam Packet Company and the ownership of the ports of Folkestone, Heysham and Newhaven, as well as the land development at Harwich. The company soon adopted the trading name of Sealink Stena Line and the ships were given the Stena prefix.

Stena Seatrader was moved to Harwich and commenced operations at the port on 2 May 1990. *St Anselm* was transferred to the Folkestone–Boulogne route to operate with *Hengist*, while *Horsa* moved to Holyhead as the second vessel on the service to Dun Laoghaire. *Fantasia* left Bremerhaven for trials in mid-February and arrived at Dover via Calais on 8 March 1990. She was now a member of the Stena fleet and entered service on a freight-only service on 11 March, before starting to take a limited number of passengers. *Fiesta* arrived at Calais in mid-May and was immediately involved in a manning dispute with the local unions.

The French vessel *Cote d'Azur* had also become involved in the dispute and was strikebound in Berth 3 at Calais. With operational berths being unavailable *Fantasia* operated an amended service to fit in between P&O sailings from Berth 6. *Fantasia* was then taken out of service for a pre-planned week-long period at Bremerhaven, where she was in dry dock for various modifications to take place. The service was operated by *St Christopher* and *Earl William* was taken out of lay-up to cover at Folkestone to enable *St Anselm* to return to the Dover–Calais service. However, after two days on service the *Earl William*'s stern door failed and she operated as a passenger vessel until 12 June. On 20 June the Port of Calais was blocked by striking French crews, forcing P&O to operate some sailings to Zeebrugge. Stena managed to operate services to Boulogne and *Fantasia* completed some non-landing cruises along the Channel until she was dry docked again at Tilbury. The French vessels were transferred from the ownership of SNCF Armement Naval to the Société Propriétaire des Navires (SPN) and Société Nouvelle d'Armement Transmanche (SNAT) was formed to operate the vessels. *Champs Elysees* was transferred to the Dieppe route and *Chartres* became the Calais–Dover Western Docks train-connected vessel.

Soon after the takeover Stena announced that it would invest around £4.5 million in the Port of Fishguard over a number of years. The money would be spent on port facilities that would enable the newly acquired *Stena Felicity* to turn around more quickly and to operate three sailings a day from 1992. In October 1990 the company announced that they would be spending 'significant sums' on upgrading the Dover fleet, replacing *Stena Antrim* with *Stena Invicta*, which had originally been a Danish Railways ferry. *Stena Challenger* was introduced to cater for the freight demands of the service, while *Fantasia* was renamed *Stena Fantasia* but she never really settled down on the route due to her lack of manoeuvrability and problems with her rudders. Problems with her bow visor later in the year brought forward her overhaul at A&P Appledore at North Shields and on her return to service she required more repairs following a number of accidents in bad weather.

Early in 1991 Stena announced that *Stena Challenger* would be withdrawn but the decision was changed and she was employed alongside the train ferry *Nord Pas de Calais* on the Dover–Dunkerque route. *Stena Fantasia* and her sister *Fiesta* undertook a major overhaul and they emerged in the now standard Stena livery. When the first year trading accounts of the company were published they showed a pre-tax loss of £28.2 million. It was felt that the company had made an excessive offer for Sealink, which was thought to be worth £180 million, not the £259 million paid by Stena for the company. In addition they had invested £178 million in new vessels, opened the Southampton–Cherbourg route and agreed to accept £200 million of Sealink's debt.

Operation Benchmark was launched to look at economies and restructuring. This resulted in the loss of 1,000 staff and the closure of the Folkestone–Boulogne route. *Stena Normandy* was transferred from Harwich to take up service on the Southampton–Cherbourg route and she was replaced at Harwich by the *Stena Britannica*. *St Christopher* was transferred to Stranraer, *Stena Cambria* to Holyhead and the *Horsa* returned to Folkestone. *St Christopher* was renamed *Stena Antrim*. *St Columba* sailed to Germany to undertake a £7 million overhaul and was replaced by *Stena Cambria*, who holed herself on 11 February 1991 and was replaced by *Stena Horsa*, which was at Birkenhead. *Stena Hibernia* returned to service at Holyhead on 14 March and was joined by *Earl William* three months later. *St Cybi* remained on the route during the summer to support the passenger vessels. *Cambridge Ferry, St Cybi, Darnia* and *Stena Antrim* saw service on the Stranraer–Larne route in 1991. *Stena Horsa* took the last sailing on the Folkestone–Boulogne route on 31 December 1991 and then sailed to Birkenhead for overhaul.

Early in 1992 it was announced that the company saved £45 million on Operation Benchmark and following losses and industrial disputes it was decided to close the Newhaven–Dieppe service. The *Versailles* sailed to Le Havre and *Champs Elysees* blocked the linkspan at Dieppe. It was thought that several companies were interested in taking over the route. *Versailles* arrived at Southampton and was renamed *Stena Londoner*, leaving Newhaven on 22 May on her first voyage. Unfortunately *Champs Elysees* was still at the linkspan and *Stena Londoner* was forced to use the freight berth. *Champs Elysees* later sailed to Southampton and was renamed *Stena Parisien*, being registered at Dieppe with a French crew. *Stena Cambria* operated from Fishguard when *Stena Felicity* went for her overhaul and the freight vessel *Auersbeg* was chartered for the service at Holyhead. A new route between Stranraer and Belfast was initiated on 1 June and in December an accident with a crane at Stranraer meant that Stena had to use the P&O berth at Cairnryan. Following the closure of the Folkestone–Boulogne route *Stena Horsa* was laid up at Milford Haven with *Earl William* and *St Cybi*. She was sold to Agoudimos Lines and renamed *Penelope A*. *Earl William* became *Pearl William* when she was sold. *Cambridge Ferry* completed her duties on the Stranraer–Larne route and sailed to Milford Haven, where she was also laid up. On 21 April 1992 she sailed to Italy and was renamed *Ita Uno*.

Chartres completed her service on the Dover–Calais route on 24 September 1993 and was sold to Agapitos Lines in December, becoming *Express Santorini*. The Italian freight vessel *Vinzia E* was chartered for three months due to heavy freight volumes on the Newhaven–Dieppe route and a new terminal was completed at Dieppe. A fast-craft service from Holyhead to Dun Laoghaire commenced on 15 July and following its success Stena announced plans for a larger vessel to operate on the route the following year. On 6 July the company announced an order for two large high-speed craft, which would be built in Finland and completed in time for the 1995 season.

Stena Challenger was transferred from Dunkerque West to the Dover–Calais route on 14 March 1994. *Stena Parisien* made the first sailing to the new terminal at Dieppe on 22 July and it was announced that *Stena Sea Lynx II* would be operating on the Newhaven–Dieppe route the following year. However, the news was rather premature and a fast craft service did not operate until 1996. As work commenced on the HSS berths at Holyhead and Dun Laoghaire Irish Ferries announced plans to introduce a new larger capacity vessel for the route from Holyhead to Dublin. The new vessel would have a capacity for 600 cars and 1,700 passengers, with a service speed of 21½ knots. The *Stena Sea Lynx II* arrived at Holyhead on 18 June and entered service four days later. *Stena Sea Lynx I* was then transferred to the Fishguard to Rosslare service. *Norrona* was chartered to cover for the 1994 winter refits at Fishguard, Holyhead and Stranraer.

In July 1995 it was announced that the partnership between Stena Sealink and the French SNAT would not continue after 31 December. SNAT would trade as SeaFrance and its ships were renamed: *Fiesta* became *Seafrance Cezanne, Cote d'Azur* was renamed *SeaFrance Renoir* and *Nord Pas de Calais* became *SeaFrance Nord Pas de Calais*. *Stena Londoner* had been transferred to the Dover–Calais route and was renamed

SeaFrance Monet. Following its grounding at Calais on 19 September *Stena Challenger* was sent to A&P on the Tyne for repairs to her hull. She emerged in the new Stena Line livery, which would be adopted by all Stena vessels and did not include the Sealink name. *Stena Sea Lynx II* carried out trials at Newhaven and Dieppe prior to service on the route. However, the new high-speed service did not commence until 1996. *Marine Evangeline* was chartered for the Newhaven–Dieppe route and *Stena Londoner* covered for the vessel refits at Fishguard and Holyhead and *Norrona* was again chartered to enable *Stena Antrim* to cover on the Holyhead and Fishguard routes. *Stena Felicity*'s charter was extended for a further twelve months to enable her to remain on the Fishguard–Rosslare service until 1997. *Stena Traveller* was employed on the Holyhead–Dublin service and the service commenced with the *Marine Evangeline* on 13 October 1995. *Stena Hibernia* was renamed *Stena Adventurer*, with the intention of moving her to the Dover–Calais service. However, this never materialised and she remained at Holyhead, operating in conjunction with the HSS.

Stena Cambria returned to Dover in January 1996 and high-speed services commenced with *Stena Lynx II* the following month. The fast-craft was moved to Gothenburg in May but was replaced the following month by the larger *Stena Lynx III*. *Stena Empereur* was introduced at Dover on 16 August as the largest vessel to operate across the Dover Strait. *Stena Challenger* was transferred from Dover to Holyhead and *Stena Voyager* was introduced on the Stranraer service on 21 July 1996. *Stena Antrim* was briefly laid up at Belfast while *Stena Caledonia* and *Stena Galloway* remained on the Stranraer–Larne route. In 1998 Stena Line's operations from Dover and Newhaven were merged with P&O European Ferries to form P&O Stena Line, with 40 per cent owned by Stena and 60 per cent by P&O. In 2002, P&O acquired all of Stena's shares in the company and became the sole owner of P&O Stena Line, which then changed its name to P&O Ferries.

In 2000 Stena acquired the Scandinavian ferry operator Scandlines AB, extending its route network and securing its presence in southern Sweden. New freight routes between the Hook of Holland and Killingholme and Rotterdam to Harwich were opened in 2002 on the company's fortieth anniversary. The Fleetwood to Larne route and three vessels operating on the service were acquired from P&O in 2004.

In November 2006 the company ordered two vessels for Stena's North Sea routes from Harwich to the Hook of Holland, with the existing ships being moved to the Kiel–Gothenburg service. The HSS *Stena Discovery* left the Harwich route in 2007 and the two new vessels were launched in 2010, with *Stena Hollandica* entering service on 16 May 2010, followed by *Stena Britannica* later that year. The Stena Belfast Terminal was moved from Albert Quay to the new Victoria Terminals 1, 2 and 4 during May 2008, reducing the crossing to Stranraer by ten minutes. In December 2010 the company acquired the Northern Irish operations of DFDS Seaways. This included the Belfast to Heysham and Birkenhead routes, two vessels from the Heysham route and two chartered vessels from the Birkenhead route. The Fleetwood to Larne route ended on 24 December 2010. *Stena Superfast VII* and *Stena Superfast VIII* were introduced in November 2011, and the company announced that the HSS service by *Stena Voyager* would end. The vessel was sold and sent to Stena Recycling for scrapping in May 2013.

As of 2019 Stena is one of the world's largest ferry operators, transporting 7.6 million passengers, 1.7 million cars and 2.1 million freight units every year. The fleet consists of thirty-eight vessels on twenty-one routes between eleven countries in Northern Europe. It has 5,600 employees from more than fifty nationalities and is a leader in sustainable shipping with over 300 implemented energy saving projects. Stena is the largest ferry operator on the Irish Sea, offering the widest choice of routes between Ireland and Britain, including Rosslare to Fishguard, Dublin to Holyhead and Belfast to Birkenhead, with a total of 224 weekly sailing options. A direct service from Rosslare to Cherbourg with three return crossings a week and two daily sailings on the Harwich to the Hook of Holland is also provided.

Routes and Ships

Baltic Sea

GDYNIA–NYNÄSHAMN
Vikingland

KARLSKRONA–GDYNIA
Stena Baltica
Stena Nordica
Stena Spirit
Stena Vision

NYNÄSHAMN–VENTSPILS
Scottish Viking
Stena Flavia

TRAVEMÜNDE–LIEPĀJA
Stena Gothica
Urd

Irish Sea

CAIRNRYAN–BELFAST
Stena Superfast VII
Stena Superfast VIII

CHERBOURG–ROSSLARE
Stena Horizon

FISHGUARD–ROSSLARE
Stena Europe

HEYSHAM–BELFAST
Stena Hiberna
Stena Scotia

HOLYHEAD–DUBLIN PORT
Stena Adventurer
Stena Superfast X

LIVERPOOL–BELFAST
Stena Forerunner
Stena Lagan
Stena Mersey

North Sea

HOEK VAN HOLLAND–HARWICH
Stena Britannica
Stena Hollandica

HOEK VAN HOLLAND–KILLINGHOLME
Stena Transit
Stena Transporter

ROTTERDAM–HARWICH
Bore Bay
Somerset

ROTTERDAM–KILLINGHOLME
Misana
Misida

Scandinavia

GÖTEBORG–FREDERIKSHAVN
Stena Danica
Stena Jutlandica
Stena Vinga

GÖTEBORG–KIEL
Stena Germanica
Stena Scandinavica

OSLO–FREDERIKSHAVN
Stena Saga

TRELLEBORG–ROSTOCK
Mecklenburg-Vorpommern
Skåne

TRELLEBORG–SASSNITZ
Sassnitz

VARBERG–GRENAA
Stena Nautica

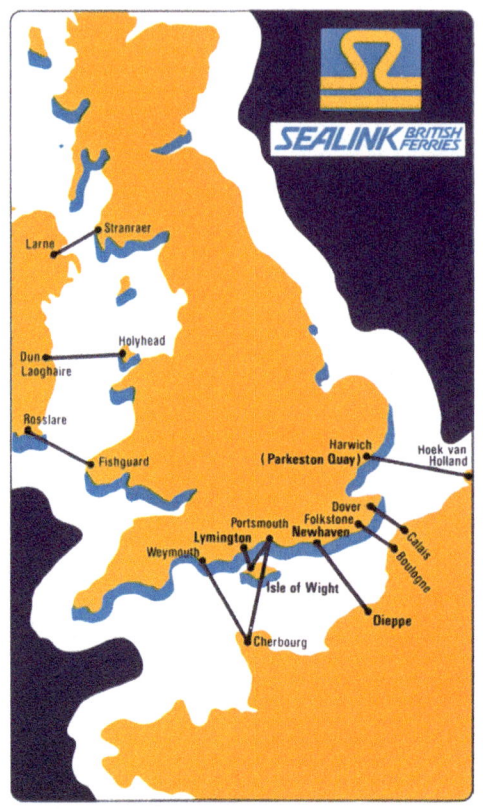

Left: Map of Sealink services.

Below: Sealink fleets.

Harwich

***Avalon**, 1963, 6,584 grt. 123x18x9m 21 knots.*
A. Stephens & Sons Limited, Linthouse. Yard No. 680 IMO 5418915

She sailed on her maiden voyage from Harwich to the Hook of Holland on 25 July 1963, replacing *Duke of York*. On 22 August 1966 she was chartered by Ellerman Wilson due to the late delivery of *Spero*. On 26 October the following year she was chartered by the Gulf Oil Corporation to convey guests to the opening of the Whiddy Island refinery by the arrival of the *Universe Ireland*. In 1974 she was made redundant by the arrival of *St Edmund* and was sent to Swan Hunter on the Tyne to be converted into a car ferry. Her lower accommodation was removed and two car decks were fitted, her superstructure was extended and a cafeteria was installed. In July 1975 she replaced *Caledonian Princess* on the Fishguard–Rosslare route, and was a relief vessel at Holyhead in January the following year when she collided with the pier at the port in fog on 17 March. She was replaced by *Dover* for three weeks. On 1 January 1979 she was transferred to Sealink UK Limited and was replaced by *Stena Normandica* and transferred to Holyhead. The following year she was laid up at Barrow and sold to Seafaith Navigation Company of Cyprus, becoming *Valon*. She was broken up at Gadani Beach, where she arrived on 22 January 1981.

Above: St George, 1968, 7,356 grt. 128x21x12m. 21 knots.
b. Swan, Hunter & Tyne Ship Building Company, Newcastle. Yard No. 2029 IMO 6810897

At the time of her delivery she was British Rail's largest ship. Transferred to Sealink UK Limited in 1979, she became relief ship in 1983, when she was replaced by *St Nicholas*. She was laid up on the River Fal and became *Patra Express* on 18 September 1984, when she was sold to Psatha Navigation Company Limited of Cyprus. In 1990 she was sold to MSJ Shipping Services, Nassau, and was renamed *Scandinavian Sky II* to replace *Scandinavian Star*. She was chartered to SeaEscape Cruises, becoming *Discovery Dawn* in 1996 and *Island Dawn* two years later. Another charter to Viva Gaming & Resorts followed when she was renamed *Texas Treasure*, operating as a casino ship at Corpus Christi and Port Aransas, Texas. She was broken up in India in 2008.

Below: St Edmund, 1974, 8,987 grt. 130.41x22.65m. 21 knots.
b. Cammell Laird & Company Limited, Birkenhead. Yard No. 1361 IMO 7340710

She was named on 13 November 1973, but her launch was delayed for twenty-four hours because of strong winds. Delivered to the British Railway Board for the Harwich–Hook of Holland service, she replaced *Avalon*. In January 1975 she was sold to Passtruck (Shipping) Company Limited, and chartered back to British Rail. On 12 May 1982 she left Harwich on charter to the Ministry of Defence to be used as a troopship in the Falklands conflict. She was later sold and operated between Ascension Islands and the Falklands in 1983 while the airport was under construction at Port Stanley, and was renamed *Karen*. On 4 July 1985 she arrived back in the United Kingdom and was laid up in the River Stour. Acquired by Cenargo Limited in 1985 she became *Scirocco*, before being renamed *Rozel* for the Poole–Channel Islands service in 1989. She became *Scirocco* again in 1993, *Santa Catherine 1* in 2004 and *Sara 3* in 2006. She was broken up in India in 2009. She is seen here with *Prinses Beatrix*.

St Nicholas, 1982, 17,043 grt. 149x16x6m. 21 knots.
b. Gotaverken Arendal A/B, Gothenburg. Yard No. 909 IMO 7901772

She was launched as *Princessan Birgitta* for the Goteborg–Frederikshavn (Sessan) Line, which was taken over by Stena A/B on 1 June 1983. Later that year she was sold to Sealink UK to replace *St George* and the chartered *Prinz Oberon*, becoming *St Nicholas*. On 27 March 1984 she arrived at Dover Harbour as the first vessel painted in the new Sealink livery. She entered service on the Harwich–Hook of Holland route on 6 June and in March 1990 she was sold to Gotland Shipping Company, and leased back for five years. In April 1990 the charter was taken over by Stena A/B, who had acquired Sealink. Following a major overhaul she emerged on 22 January 1991 as *Stena Normandy* and operated her final sailing on the Harwich–Hook of Holland route on 22 June that year before being transferred to the Southampton–Cherbourg route. She remained on that service until December 1996, when the charter with Stena A/B expired, and was then laid up at Dunkerque. This was followed by a charter to Tallink, Estonia, in January 1997, when she was renamed *Normandy*. On completion of the charter at the end of the year she was registered in Ireland and was chartered to Irish Ferries for the Rosslare–Pembroke route. In 1999 she was sold to Irish Ferries by Gotland and sent to Poland for a major overhaul and refurbishment. Side sponsons were also added to her hull for improved stability. She was replaced by the *Oscar Wilde* in 2007 and was sold to the Singapore-based oil service company Equinox Offshore Accommodation in January 2008. However, she was chartered by Ferrimaroc in March for the Almeria–Nador service for the summer season and arrived at Singapore on 19 October for conversion. The work did not commence and she was abandoned at the berth with her condition declining rapidly. On 31 October 2012 she left Singapore and was broken up in India.

Above: *Essex Ferry*, 1957, 3,243 grt. 122x19x4m. 13 knots.
b. John Brown & Company Limited, Clydebank. Yard No. 694 IMO 5106653
  She was delivered in January 1957 and was designed for service in the Irish Sea if required. On 23 May 1972, with *Norfolk Ferry*, she carried new CIE rolling stock from Holyhead to Dublin. In 1982 she was laid up with *Norfolk Ferry* and was sold to Medway Secondary Metals to be broken up. She arrived at Rainham on 29 April 1983 and was cut down into a pontoon to assist in the salvage work on the capsized Norwegian oil rig platform *Alexander Kielland*. She was towed to Norway in June 1983 and was broken up when the work was completed.

Below: *Cambridge Ferry*, 1963, 3,294 grt. 123x19x6m. 13 ½ knots.
b. Hawthorn, Leslie Limited, Newcastle. Yard No. 754 IMO 6400044
  On 12 January, 7 March and 17 July 1972 she made three voyages from Holyhead to Dublin with new rolling stock for CIE. In 1977 her stern was modified to enable her to berth at Dunkirk and her top deck was extended to carry twenty-five more vehicles. In 1982 she was placed on reserve and was later transferred to the Dover–Dunkirk route. On 31 January 1987 she took the last Harwich–Zeebrugge train ferry sailing and was transferred to the Dover–Zeebrugge route. In 1988 she was laid up on the River Fal but spent some time on the Rosslare route when *St Brendan* was out of service. She also acted as standby vessel to *Stena Felicity* on the Fishguard–Rosslare service in 1991 and was sold to Maltese interests in 1992, becoming *Ita Uno* for an Italy–Albanian service. Renamed *Siri* in 1993 she was sold to Turkish ship-breakers in 2003 and broken up.

Above: *Cambridge Ferry* laid up on the River Fal.

Below: *Speedlink Vanguard*, 1973, 8,104 grt. 115x11x6m. 18 knots.
b. A. Vuyk & Zonen Scheepswerven BV, Capelle an der Ijssel. Yard No. 864 IMO 7325241

Launched on 16 June 1973 as *Stena Shipper* for Stena A/B, she was chartered to the Union Steam Ship Company as *Union Wellington*. She was sold to Greek interests in 1977 and renamed *Alpha Express*. Lengthened, with sponsons, bow, stern doors and bow thruster fitted, she became *Stena Shipper* in 1980 with Stena Cargo Line A/B and was chartered to Northern Coasters Limited, London, before being re-chartered to Sealink UK. On 4 May she arrived at Smiths Dock, Middlesbrough, and was converted into a train ferry. New funnels were fitted and she was renamed *Speedlink Vanguard* for the Harwich–Zeebrugge and Harwich–Dunkirk West services. On 19 December 1982 she collided with the *European Gateway*, which sank, with a loss of six lives. She made her final Harwich–Zeebrugge sailing on 29 January 1987 and was renamed *Caribe Express* and *Stena Shipper* the following year. In 1989 she operated for Truckline as *Kirk Shipper*, and later *Normandie Shipper* for the Portsmouth–Caen–Ouistreham service. She became *Bona Vista* in 1999 and *Boa Vista* in 2001. Acquired by Thraki Shipping in 2007 and renamed *Birlik 1*, she was broken up at Turkey in 2013.

17

Sea Freightliner 1, **1968, 4,034 grt. 118x16x6m. 13½ knots.**
b. J. Redhead & Sons Limited (Swan Hunter Group) Yard No. 621 IMO 6803416
   Launched for the Harwich–Zeebrugge service as the first cellular container ship in the United Kingdom, she arrived at Kaohsiung on 4 May 1987 and was broken up.

Zeeland Steam Ship Company

Koningin Wilhelmina, **1960, 6,228 grt. 120x17m. 21 knots.**
b. De Merwede Shipyard, Hardinxveld, Netherlands. Yard No. 548 IMO 5192987
   She was sold to Ventouris Ferries in 1978 and was renamed *Captain Constantinos*, *Panagia Tinou* in 1981, *Artemis* in 1994 and *Temis* in 2001, when she was broken up in India.

Koningin Juliana, 1968, 6,682 grt. 131x20x5m. 21 knots.
b. Cammell Laird & Company Limited, Birkenhead Yard No. 1331 IMO 6808806
   She was sold and became *Moby Prince* in 1985 and on 10 April 1991 she collided with the tanker *Agip Abruzzo* and a fire engulfed the vessel. The flames quickly spread around the ship, causing the death of 140 people. A young ship's boy was the only survivor of the tragedy. On 28 May 1998 the ship's hull sank in dock at Livorno and was later re-floated and towed to Turkey, where it was broken up.

Above left: *Princes Beatrix,* 1978, 9,238 grt. 132x24x5m.
b. Verolme Scheepswerf Heusden, Holland. Yard No. 959 IMO 7637149
   She became *Duc de Normandie* in 1986, *Wisteria* in 2005 and *Vronskiy* in 2013.

Above right: *Koningin Beatrix,* 1986, 32,189 grt. 162x25m. 20 knots.
b. Van der Giessen de Noord, Netherlands. Yard No. 935 IMO 8416308
   She became *Stena Baltica* in 2002 and SNAV *Adriatico* in 2013.

Edith, 1960, 214 grt. 34x9x2m. 9 knots.
b. J. S. White & Company Limited, Cowes. Passengers: 475. IMO 5619704

She was sold to the Whitehorse Group in 1984 for use as a floating restaurant and bar, but has been undergoing a slow conversion into a houseboat at Great Wakering in Essex.

Dover

Shepperton Ferry, 1935, 2,839 grt. 105.7x18.5m. 16½ knots.
b. Swan, Hunter & Wigham Richardson Limited, Newcastle. Yard No. 1446. IMO 5322544. Twin screw, 2x2 turbines, 4,500 ihp, four automatic Yarrow boilers by Parsons Marine Steam Turbine Company.

She operated as a minelayer in the Straits of Dover as HMS *Shepperton* in 1939 and assisted in the evacuation of the Channel Islands in 1940. Following this she reverted back to minelaying for a short period before transferring to the Stranraer–Larne route. At the end of hostilities she reopened the Dover–Dunkirk route on 19 February 1946, and was converted to burn oil later that year. She relieved the *Caledonian Princess* on the Stranraer–Larne service in 1964, during her annual overhaul. Her final sailing took place on 25 August 1972 and she was then laid up at Wellington Dock, Dover. She left Dover in tow on 12 September and arrived at Bilbao on 19 September, where she was broken up.

Above: *Twickenham Ferry,* 1934, 2,839 grt. 105.7x18.5m. 16½ knots.
b. Swan, Hunter & Wigham Richardson Limited, Newcastle. Yard No. 1446 IMO 5371478

She was designed and built as a train and car ferry with accommodation for twelve wagon sleeping cars or forty rail wagons, plus twenty-five cars in the upper deck garage. Delivered for the Dover–Dunkirk service, the introduction of which was delayed because of engineering problems at Dover, she operated the first Dover–Dunkirk night crossing on 6 October and was transferred to SA de Nav. Angleterre-Loraine-Alsace (ALA) ownership. On 25 August 1939 the service was suspended and she was converted into a minelayer, becoming HMS *Twickenham*. In 1940 she operated on the English Channel and was later transferred to Stranraer–Larne. In July 1944 she was fitted with large gantries, an eighty-four-trolley crane and a stern ramp to enable her and her two sisters to deliver railway stock to places where the infrastructure had been destroyed. In 1945 she returned to ALA ownership and was converted to burn oil two years later. In January 1974 she was replaced by *St Eloi* but continued in service to complete a large order for railway wagons for Yugoslavia. Her final sailing was on 5 May and she was sold later that month, being broken up by Steelnorte SA at San Esteban de Pravia.

Below: *Saint Eloi,* 1975, 4,649 grt 115x18x11m. 19½ knots.
b. Cantieri Navali di Pietra, Ligure. Yard No. 12 IMO 7207451

She was launched as *St Eloi* on 1 June 1973. As her builders went into liquidation, *Twickenham Ferry* was retained in service. She was eventually delivered in 1975 and in 1977 ALA became a French-operated wholly owned subsidiary of British Rail. In 1988 she introduced a night freight service on the Folkestone–Boulogne route and acted as a relief vessel on other routes, becoming *Channel Entente* in 1990. She was acquired by the Isle of Man Steam Packet on 8 December 1990 and renamed *King Orry*, operating on Irish Sea services from Heysham and Liverpool to Douglas. In 1998 she was sold, becoming *Moby Love*. On 1 April 2019 she was renamed *Azores Express*.

Channel Entente.

King Orry.

Moby Love.

Invicta, 1939, 4,178 grt. 117.19x15.27m. 22 knots.
b. William Denny & Brothers Limited, Dumbarton. Yard No. 1344. Twin screw, 2x2 two stage Parsons turbines, 1,100 nhp, two Yarrow boilers by builder. Yard No. 1344 IMO 5162217

She was ordered in 13 February 1939 for the 'Golden Arrow' service to replace Canterbury, and operated one return trip each day. She was launched on 14 December and delivered on 1 July the following year. However, she was laid up at anchor for ten months before being requisitioned by the Admiralty and was fitted with de-gaussing equipment by Barclay Curle. She was commissioned on 3 June 1941 and transported Canadian troops to Dieppe during Operation Jubilee. In June 1944 she participated in the Normandy invasion and was decommissioned in December the following year. In 1946 she was operating on Southern Region services, replacing *Canterbury* on the 'Golden Arrow' service on 15 October. She held the distinction of being the largest English Channel ship until the arrival of *Princess Paola* in 1966. During her 1947 overhaul her original stabilisers were finally fitted and on 1 January 1948 she was transferred to the British Transport Commission. Early in 1965 she introduced the new British Rail livery on the Dover–Calais service. In July 1972 she was replaced on the 'Golden Arrow' service by the *Maid of Orleans*, taking her final sailing on 8 August before being laid up at Newhaven. On 21 September she was towed by *Michel Petersen* to Rotterdam, where she was broken up.

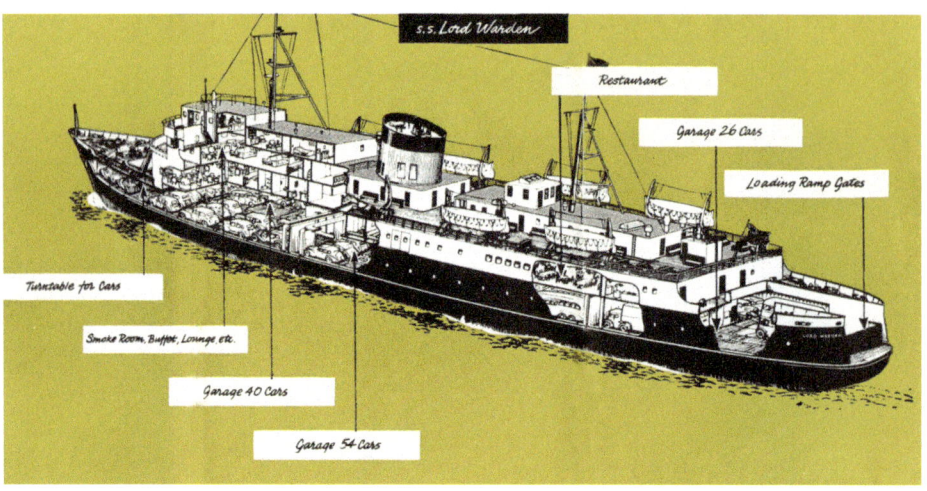

Lord Warden, 1952, 3,333 grt. 110.37x18.5m. 20 knots.
b. William Denny & Brothers Limited, Dumbarton. Yard No. 1455 IMO 5212191

She was launched on 14 December 1951 as British Railway's first designed car ferry, with electrically operated stern doors. She sailed on her maiden voyage from Dover to Boulogne on 16 June 1952. However, as the facilities were not ready cars were craned onboard at Dover but driven off at Boulogne. On 15 June 1953 she was present at the Coronation Spithead Review, prior to the ramp becoming available at Dover. In 1956 her funnel was fitted with a new top to alleviate fumes when going astern. In May and October 1968 she was used as a 'Back Britain' exhibition ship at Copenhagen, Gothenburg, Stockholm, Helsinki and Oslo. On 7 April 1971 she operated on the Holyhead–Dun Laoghaire route when *Holyhead Ferry 1* was sent to Fishguard. On 1 January 1979 she was transferred to Sealink UK Limited and after operating at Holyhead she was sent to Newhaven and laid up. On 19 November she was sold to Ahmed Mohamed Baaboud of Jeddah, becoming *Al Zaher*. Following work by Thornycroft she left Southampton on 2 January 1980 for Jeddah, carrying a cargo of sheep on the Port Sudan–Jeddah section of the voyage. On 25 April 1981 she arrived at Gadani Beach and was broken up by Karim Shipbreaking Industries.

Maid of Kent, 1959, 4,413 grt. 113.7x18.4m. 20 knots.
b. William Denny & Brothers Limited, Dumbarton. Yard No. 1492 IMO 5217531

Maid of Kent was launched as a stern-loading car ferry for the Dover–Boulogne service on 27 November 1958. On 10 September 1973 she damaged her bow at Boulogne and cars were craned ashore prior to her being towed back for repairs. She operated on the Stranraer–Larne service in 1975, while *Antrim Princess* was away on overhaul. In March the following year *Avalon* was damaged on the Holyhead–Dun Laoghaire service, *Dover* was moved from Fishguard–Rosslare and *Maid of Kent* was sent to replace her. On 1 January 1979 she was taken over by Sealink UK Limited. On 2 October 1981 she took her final sailing to Cherbourg, followed by another to Jersey, and was then laid up at Newhaven. She left Newhaven on 10 April 1982 and was broken up at San Esteban de Pravia by Desguaces Aviles SA.

Above: Normannia, 1952, 3,543 grt. 94.24x14.69x5.33m. 19 knots.
b. William Denny & Brothers, Dumbarton. Twin screw, two Pametrada turbines, 8,000 shp, two Foster-Wheeler boilers by builder. Yard No. 1454 IMO 5256408

She sailed on her maiden voyage from Southampton to Le Havre on 3 March 1952, replacing *Hantonia.* The following year she operated on the Harwich–Hook of Holland route to replace the damaged *Duke of York,* and in 1962 she was converted to a stern-loading vehicle ferry on the Tyne. In 1965 she inaugurated the new car ferry service from Holyhead to Dub Laoghaire following the delay of the delivery of *Holyhead Ferry 1.* In the following years she saw service as relief vessel on most cross-Channel and Irish Sea routes, finally arriving at Gijon on 6 December 1978 to be broken up.

Opposite page top: St Patrick, 1948, 3,482 grt. 97.9x14.69m. 20 knots.
b. Cammell Laird & Company Limited, Birkenhead. Twin screw, 2x2 Parsons steam turbines, 8,500 bhp, three Babcock & Wilcox boilers by builder. Yard No. 1183 ID 530658

Launched on 20 May 1947, she sailed on her maiden voyage on the Weymouth to the Channel Islands daylight route on 4 February 1948. She was laid up at Fishguard in October that year for the winter. On 1 November 1948 the Great Western Railway Marine Division was split in two, with Weymouth going to the Southern Region. On 1 January 1950 the Port of Fishguard and the ships were transferred to the London Midland Region. On 17 September 1950 she was blown across St Helier Harbour in a gale and was grounded on Rats Corner. She was soon floated and later went to Penarth for repairs. Later that year she was owned by the British Transport Commission. In 1960/61 she became a one-class vessel for the Channel Islands route and replaced *Brittany* on the Jersey–St Malo service in 1963. In 1964 she was converted into a side-loading car ferry and was placed on the Folkestone–Boulogne service the following year. In 1971 she was laid up at Newhaven and was sold to Gerasimos S. Fetouris, becoming *Thermopylae* the following year. She was acquired by Agapitos Brothers of Piraeus in 1973 and renamed *Agopitos 1.* Laid up in 1976, she was broken up at Perama in 1980.

Below left and right: *Holyhead Ferry 1/Earl Leofric,* 1965, 3,879 grt. 112.47x17.43m. 21 knots.
b. Hawthorn Leslie Limited, Newcastle. Yard No. 757 IMO 6508470

She entered service on the Holyhead–Dun Laoghaire route in 1965. Because of rail bridge repairs sailings were cancelled and she operated on the service for the first time in over a year on 31 January 1972. She was transferred to the Weymouth–Channel Islands service in place of the damaged *Caesarea* on 2 March 1973 and was converted to operate on the English Channel by Swan Hunter on the Tyne in 1976. She replaced *Artevelde* at Dover on 23 September 1976 and took twenty hours to complete a Boulogne–Dover sailing in severe gale conditions on 14 October 1976. Converted to a drive through vehicle vessel in 1976, she was renamed *Earl Leofric*. She was at sea for ten hours in a gale in the Irish Sea on 28 January 1978. On a voyage from Calais to Folkestone on 26 February 1979 she collided with the pier and was out of service for two weeks. On 27 October 1980 she was replaced by *St Anselm*, was laid up at Newhaven and briefly stood in for *Earl Siward*. She was sold on 30 May 1981 and broken up in Spain.

Above: *Dover/Earl Siward,* 1965, 3,602 grt. 112.47x16.76x10.52m. 19 ½ knots.
b. Swan, Hunter & Wigham Richardson Limited, Newcastle. Yard No. 2013 IMO 6510784 Twin screw, two turbines, 12,000 bhp, two boilers by Wallsend Slipway & Engineering Company.

She entered service on the Dover–Calais route and when *Vortigern* was delivered in 1969 she was transferred to the Holyhead–Dun Laoghaire service. On 1 June 1969 she carried 200 Ford cars from Preston to Boulogne. While operating on the Newhaven–Dieppe route on 2 November 1972 she was at sea for twenty-two hours due to fog and inoperative bow doors. Renamed *Earl Siward* in 1977 following conversion to a drive-through vehicle ferry, she replaced *Avalon* on the Holyhead–Dun Laoghaire service. In 1982 she was sold to Sol Ferries of Cyprus and renamed *Sol Express*. Four years later she was acquired by the Quadrini Group, Chanson Lines Limited, for conversion into a floating nightclub and arrived on the Tyne on 18 April 1986, becoming *Tuxedo Royale* and replacing *Tuxedo Express* (*Caledonian Princess*). She later moved to Middlesbrough as a nightclub and entered the National Historic Ships register in 2016 but was badly damaged by fire on 1 June 2017.

Below: Sol Express.

Stena Fantasia, 1980, 8,919 grt. 164x16x8m. 21 knots.
b. Kockums Varv, Malmö. Yard No. 569 IMO 7814462

Delivered to R/A Nordo, Malmö, as *Scandinavia* for a service from Jugoslavia to Syria, she was sold to Navigation Maritime Bulgare in 1982 and renamed *Tzarevetz*, before being taken over by Sealink involving an exchange between the two Seafreight ships. She was renamed *Fiesta* and temporarily employed on a service to Nigeria. Converted into a vehicle carrier with her sister by Bremer Vulcan and Lloyd Werft during 1989/90, she became *Fantasia* and was placed on the Dover–Calais route. Following an overhaul in 1990 she emerged as *Stena Fantasia* and because of problems berthing the two vessels an extra propeller was added between the twin rudders and another bow thruster was fitted. She became P&OSL *Canterbury* in 1998, P&O *Canterbury* in 2002, *Alkmini A* and *Wawel* in 2004.

Stena Challenger, 1991, 18,523 grt. 154x24x6m. 17½ knots.
b. Fosen Mek, Versteder, Fosen. Yard No. 20 IMO 8917388

Delivered to Sealink Stena Line, she was operated on the Dover–Dunkirk West route. She was later purchased by the government of Canada in 2001 to operate on the North Sydney, Nova Scotia and Port aux Basques, Newfoundland and Labrador route, becoming *Leif Ericson.*

Dover/Folkestone–Ostend

Ostend–Dover.

Above: Koning Albert, **1947, 3,710 grt.**
b. Cockerill-Ougrée, Hoboken. Yard No. 726 IMO 5192937
   She was withdrawn in 1973 and broken up in Ghent, where she arrived on 23 May 1978.

Below: Roi Leopold III, **1956, 3,794 grt.**
b. Cockerill-Ougrée, Hoboken. Yard No. 777 IMO 5298808
   Withdrawn in 1976 and sold to Panamanian interests in 1978, becoming *Najd*, she arrived at Gadani Beach on 15 March 1987 and was broken up by the World Marine Shipbuilding & Trading Company.

Above: *Artevelde,* 1958, 2,812 grt.
b. Cockerill-Ougrée, Hoboken. Yard No. 794 IMO 5025586
   In 1976 she was sold to Greek interests and renamed *Algaion.* She was laid up in 1995 to be rebuilt for day cruising, and it was intended to rename her *Kallisti*. However, on 19 February 1996 she caught fire and while being towed from the dock area she sank at Atalanti Island.

Below: *Koningin Fabiola,* 1962, 4,727 grt. 117x15.84m. 20 knots.
b. J. Boel & Zonen Shipyard, Temse, Belgium. Yard No. 1391 IMO 5192963
   She was named after the queen of Belgium and was the first vessel ordered from Boel at Temse, operating on Belgian Marine's Ostend–Dover passenger and car ferry service. She became *Olympia* and *Lydia* in 1985, *Ephesus* in 1995, *Bergama* in 1996 and *Bosporus* in 1998. She was sold and broken up at Aliaga in 2004.

Above: *Koningin Fabiola* became *Lydia*.

Below: *Prins Philippe*, 1973, 5,071 grt. 118mx19m.
b. Boelwerf Vlaanderen, Temse. Yard No. 1476 IMO 7305514

She operated between Dover and Ostend until 1986, when she was sold to Moby Lines, where she was renamed *Moby Love*. In 1993 she was acquired by Ventouris Sea Lines, becoming *Panagia Tinou 2* until 1998, when she was purchased by Agapitos Express Ferries and renamed *Express Athina*. She was transferred to operate out of Rafina to Mykonos in 2005 when *Hellas Ferries* became *Hellenic Seaways*, and she received the company's new blue hull colours. She sailed out of Rafina in competition with a previous sister, *Prince Laurent*, which became *Superferry II*, operating for Strintzis/Blue Star Ferries. In 2007 she was sold to SAOS Ferries and was renamed *Express Limnos*. She arrived at Aliaga on 7 November 2011 and was broken up.

Above: *Prince Laurent,* 1974, 5,052 grt. 118x19x12m. 22 knots.
b. Boelwerf SA, Temse. Yard No. 1477 IMO 7346221

She entered service on the official opening of the new Admiralty Pier linkspan at the Western Docks, Dover, on 28 June 1974. An agreement was reached with Townsend Thoresen on 25 October 1985 and this excluded Sealink UK Limited. The arrangement was transferred to P&O European Ferries in October 1985 and all Ostend vessels received the Townsend Thoresen orange hulls and the trading name. A new livery was applied to the Ostend vessels during 1987/88, and in 1991 *Prince Laurent* was laid up. She was sold to the Strintzis Line the following year, becoming *Ionian Express*. She was renamed *Superferry II* in 1993 and was sold in 2011, retaining the same name.

Below: *Prinses Paola,* 1966, 3,388 grt. 117x16x5m. 24 knots.
b. Cockerill-Ougrée, Hoboken. Yard No. 836 IMO 6608294

She was delivered as the last conventional passenger vessel to be built for the Ostend service and sailed on her maiden voyage on 14 June 1966. In March 1988 she was sold to Sea Venture Cruises, renamed *Tropicana* and sailed to Perama to be rebuilt as a cruise ship/casino. She operated from Miami and Port Everglades in 1988/89 and was chartered to Seascape to operate cruises from St Petersburg. In 1990 she was renamed *Sea Palace* and operated from Freeport, Texas, as a floating casino. On 17 April 1991 she was arrested at Houston and was later sold to Winston Cruise Lines of Nassau, becoming *Saint Lucie*. She was out of service for two years and following renovations she returned to Florida in December 1994. In January 1995 she was acquired by Jubilee, Bahamas Incorporated, becoming *Tropicana,* again to operate day cruising from Miami and occasional trips between Miami and Freeport. The following year she was laid up in Brooklyn and later Charleston, South Carolina, and Freeport, Bahamas. On 2 November 2006 she took on bunkers at Gibraltar following a crossing from Freeport en route to Alang to be broken up.

Above: *Prinses Paola* in Townsend Thoresen colours.

Below: *Reine Astrid,* 1958, 3,795 grt. 114x15.2m. 23 knots.
b. Cockerill-Ougrée, Hoboken. Yard No. 785 IMO 5292452
   She was launched on 25 July 1957 for cross-Channel services from Ostend to Dover. In 1985 she was hulked at Flushing.

35

Above: *Roi Baudouin,* 1965, 3,241 grt. 118x16x5m.
b. Cockerill-Ougrée, Hoboken. Yard No. 828 IMO 6510851

Her maiden voyage was on 13 June 1965 on the Ostend–Dover service. She also operated from Ostend to Parkeston Quay, taking the final sailing to Harwich on 10 September 1973. In July 1982 she was laid up at Ostend and was later chartered to Sealink UK Limited for the Dover–Calais and Folkestone–Boulogne routes. Sold in 1983 to the Ventouris Group, she was renamed *Georgios B* and later *Georgios Express*. In 1995 she was laid up at Piraeus, returning to service for a short time for Aghios Georgios Ferries in 2000. Laid up later that year, she was sold to Greek shipbreakers. In 2008 she was re-sold to Indian breakers, leaving Elefsis under tow on 24 March 2009, and was broken up at Aliaga, Turkey.

Below: *Prinses Maria Esmeralda,* 1975, 5,635 grt. 118x21x6m. 22 knots.
b. Cockerill Yards, Hoboken. Yard No. 877 IMO 7357555

On 30 May 1979 she was in collision with the German coaster *Eleonora*, near the Goodwin Sands, which sank within fifteen minutes. An extra lorry deck was inserted in 1986 by her builders at Hoboken. In 1994 she was laid up at Ostend and was sold to Denval Marine, becoming *Wisteria* to operate on the Trieste–Koper–Bar–Durrës service. In 1995 she was chartered to Cotunav and commenced service between Tunis–Genoa–Naples, and became *Beni Ansar* in 1997 and *Wisteria* again the following year. In 2000 she was sold to Lignes Maritimes du Detroit and was once again renamed *Beni Ansar* for the Almería–Nador route. On 15 November 2007 she was beached at Alang and broken up.

Above: Wisteria.

Below: *Princess Marie Christine*, 1975, 5,543 grt. 118.42x19.99m. 22 knots.
b. Cockerill Yards, Hoboken. Yard No. 878 IMO 7357567

She was launched on 8 September 1975 for the Ostend to Dover passenger and roll-on/roll-off car and commercial vehicle ferry service. On 27 October 1976 she suffered extensive damage following an engine room fire, and on 13 September 1981 her engines failed, but she was back in service on 2 October. In 1985 she had an extra lorry deck fitted by Boel Shipyards at Temse and the company entered into negotiations with Townsend Thoreson to provide services from Dover. The agreement was passed to P&O European Ferries in 1987, and the ships were painted in orange livery. In 1987–88 another new livery was adopted, along with a fourth seven years later in 1991. The agreement with P&O was not renewed in 1993 and from January the following year the company was known as Oostende Lines, working in conjunction with Sally Line, operating from Ramsgate. In 1997 she was laid up and sold to Denval Marine Consultants the following year, becoming *Primrose* and operating for TransEuropa Shipping Lines between Ramsgate and Ostend. On 17 June 2009 she left Ostend on charter to Comarit for service between Spain and Morocco, and France and Morocco. She returned from her charter in September 2009 and commenced a service between Piombino and Portoferraio in June 2010. She was renamed *Elegant 1* for her delivery voyage to Alang, where she was broken up in 2011.

Above: **Prins Albert**, 1978, 6,019 grt. 118x20x6m. 22 knots.
b. Cockerill Yards, Hoboken. Yard No. 887 IMO 7613882

In January 1986 she entered her builders for extensive work to be carried out and this was completed on 17 May, when she left the yard. In May 1998 she was sold to Hawthorn Shipping of Limassol, was renamed *Eurovoyager* and was chartered to the Sally Line (later TransEuropa Shipping Lines) for service between Ostend and Ramsgate. From June to 2 September 2010 she operated between Almería and Al Hoceima, and from Algeciras to Tangier in 2011. On 30 April 2012 she was beached at Aliaga and broken up.

Below: **Prinses Stephanie**, 1981, 329 grt. 27x10m. 43 knots.
b. Boeing Jetfoil Industries, Seattle, Washington. Yard No. 20 IMO 7932070

She was sold and renamed *Adler Wizard* in 1998, *Thor Simba* and *Seajet Kristen* in 1999 and *Seven Island Yume* in 2001.

Above: *Princesse Clementine,* 1981, 329 grt. 27x10m. 43 knots.
b. Boeing Jetfoil Industries, Seattle, Washington. Yard No. 19. IMO 7932068
   She became *Adler Blizzard* in 1998, *Alderney Blizzard*, *Seajet Kara* and *Seven Island Niji* in 2002. She began operating for Tokai Kisen Company Limited, Japan, in 2018.

Below: *Stena Nautica/Reine Astrid,* 1975, 5,443 grt.
b. Rickmers Werft, Bremerhaven. Yard No. 382 IMO 7360629
   Delivered as *Stena Nordica*, she became *Hellas* in 1978, *Stena Nordica*, *Hellas* and *Stena Nordica* in 1979, *Stena Nautica* in 1982, *Reine Astrid* in 1983 and *Moby Kiss* and *Al Mansour* in 1997. She arrived at Aliaga on 12 August 2015 and was broken up.

SNCF

Cote D'Azur, 1951, 4,037 grt. 111x15x5m. 22 knots.
b. Forges et Chantiers de la Méditerranée SA, Le Havre. IMO 5081217
   She was sold in 1973, becoming *Azur* and *Marie F*, and was broken up in Murcia later that year.

Above: *Chantilly,* 1966, 3,400 grt. 109.9x17.8m.
b. Dubigeon-Normandie, Nantes-Chantenay. Yard No. 822 IMO 6601997

Société Nationale des Chemins de fer Français. Twin reversible screw, two Pielstick Vee oil, two twelve-cylinder, 9,300 bhp engines by Ateliers & Chantiers de Nantes.

She was launched on 9 November 1965 for cross-Channel services from France to England. In 1987 she was sold and renamed *Olympia*, followed by *Europa Link* in 1990, *Baltavia* in 1993 and *Al Salam 93* in 1996. She was broken up in 2003.

Below: *Compiegne,* 1958, 3,467 grt. 115.03x18.35x6.4m. 20 knots.
b. Chargeurs Réunis Loire-Normandie, Rouen. Twin screw, controllable pitch, oil, 2 sixteen-cylinder Pielstick 4s.sa, 9,000 shp by Soc. Gen. de Construction Mechanique. Yard No. 310 IMO 5077905

SNCF became the owners/managers in 1960 and in February 1964 she carried out tests at Newhaven, prior to the introduction of *Villandry*. From 1978 she operated summer services on the Dover–Boulogne route and was laid up on 7 October 1980. She came out of lay up in February 1981 to cover the overhauls of *Chartres* and *Chantilly*. Following these duties she was sold to Strintzi Lines Shipping SA, Piraeus, and was renamed *Ionian Glory* for the Ancona–Brindisi–Corfu–Igoumenitsa–Patras service. In 1990 she became *Queen Verginia* and operated between Piraeus and Haifa. She was renamed *Freedom I* in 1990, *Katerina* in 1994, *Al Amirah* in 1995 and later became *Al Ameerah*. She was taken off the register in 2010, and it is reported that she was broken up two years later.

Above and below: *Villandry*, 1964, 3,444 grt. 105x18x4m. 21 knots.
b. Dubigeon-Normandie SA, Nantes. Yard No. 809 IMO 6503597

She was sold to Agapitos Brothers in 1985, renamed *Olympia,* and was re-sold to Ionian Lines Shipping of Piraeus the following year, becoming *Delos.* In 1998 she became *Adrina Lestari* and was broken up later that year.

Above and below: *Valencay*, 1965, 3,430 grt. 105x17.1m.
b. Atlantique (Penhoët-Loire), St Nazaire, France. Yard No. E23 IMO 6508157

She was launched on 6 February 1965 to be employed on cross-Channel services from France to England. She was sold in 1984, becoming *Eptanisos*, followed by *Pollux* in 2000 and *Pollux 1* in 2003. She was broken up at Gadani Beach in 2004.

Above and below: *Chartres,* 1973, 4,800 grt. 115.4x19.23x6.18m. 20½ knots.
b. Dubigeon-Normandie SA, Nantes. Twin screw, two sixteen-cylinder Pielstick Vee oil, 4s.sa, 16,000 bhp by Chantiers de l'Atlantique. Yard No. 137 IMO 7330040

Delivered for the Dover–Dunkirk and summer Dover–Calais routes, she was transferred to the Dover–Dunkirk West route with the delivery of the *Cote d'Azur* in 1981 and operated with *Senlac* and *Valencay* on the Newhaven service in 1983. She reverted back to the Dover–Dunkirk route in 1986 and on a voyage to Dieppe on 25 January 1990 she suffered engine and steering gear problems and sustained heavy damage on arrival at the port. In 1991 she was chartered by the French Government to bring back military equipment at the end of the Gulf War. On a voyage from Newhaven on 25 January 1990 she experienced a Force 11/12 gale, with waves up to 70 feet high, which caused a total electrical failure with both main engines coming to a halt. The ship's master, Captain Yves Lerouvrer, sent out a mayday call and a lifeboat and coastguard helicopter were sent from the United Kingdom. A French Navy frigate and a cargo ship were also diverted towards her. However, the main engines were restarted after three quarters of an hour and she was able to resume her journey to Dieppe. As she entered the harbour she was blown against the pier, resulting in a gash some 150 feet long below the waterline. With the help and assistance of tugs and the seamanship skills of the captain and crew she made it alongside the quay and the passengers were discharged. Following repairs she was placed on the Dover Western Dock–Calais service. Her rails were removed in 1993 and she became *Express Santorini* later that year, followed by *Al Salmy 4* in 2016.

Above left and right: *Cote D'Azur,* 1981, 8,862 grt. 130x23x7m. 18 knots.
b. Soc. Nouvelle des Ateliers & Chantiers du Havre. Yard No. 236 IMO 7920534

Delivered for the Calais–Dover service replacing *Chartres*, on 5 August 1982 she collided with *Chantilly* 4 miles off Calais in good visibility. Her bow visor was damaged and when it was later welded she continued in service as a stern-loader. She also served on the Boulogne–Dover service with Sealink partners. Her ownership was transferred to SPN in 1990, with Stena holding a 49 per cent interest, and from 1996 the service was marketed as SeaFrance. She was rebuilt in 1996, becoming *SeaFrance Renoir*. In 2011 she was renamed *Eastern Light* and was beached at Alang on 9 November 2011 and broken up.

Below: Seafrance Renoir.

Above and below: *Champs Elysées/Stena Parisien,* 1984, 9,069 grt. 130x25x5m.
b. Dubigeon-Normandie SA, Nantes. Yard No. 167 IMO 8208763

She sailed on her maiden voyage on 4 October 1984 from Calais to Dover, but was designed and built for the Dover–Boulogne route, replacing *Chantilly*. On 3 June 1992 she was renamed *Stena Parisien* while on charter to Sealink Stena Line for the Newhaven–Dieppe service. She was rebuilt in 1997 with the addition of a stern duck tail sponson and was renamed *Seafrance Manet*. In 2008 she was renamed *Stena Navigator,* was registered in London for Stena's Belfast to Stranraer service, and was sold to Eurolineas Maritima SAL (Balearia), Spain, becoming *Daniya* in 2012. She was renamed *Poeta Lopez Anglada* in November 2013.

Seafrance Manet.

Versailles/Stena Londoner, 1974, 6,737 grt. 125x12x5m. 22 knots.

b. Brodogradiliste, Trogir, Jugoslavia. Yard No. 163 IMO 7321661

Launched as *Stena Nordica* for Stena A/S, she entered service as *Stena Danica*. She was rebuilt in 1977 to allow vehicles to be carried on both decks, and in 1981 she became *Stena Nordica* again. She was renamed *Stena Nautica* and *Reine Astrid* two years later and then *Stena Nautica* again when the Regie voor Maritiem Transport Ostend–Dover charter ended in 1986. Chartered to SNCF in 1988, she was renamed *Versailles/Stena Londoner* and fitted with a stern ramp for the Dover–Calais service. In 1992 she became *Stena Londoner*, for the Newhaven–Dieppe service. She was renamed *Seafrance Monet* in 1996 and operated on the Calais–Dover service. On 11 September 2009 she became *Volcan De Tacande* and arrived at Aliaga on 11 September 2005 to be broken up.

Nord Pas De Calais, 1987, 13,727grt 159x23x6m. 21 knots.
b. Chantiers du Nord et de la Méditerranée SA, Dunkirk. Yard No. 325 IMO 8512152

She operated on the Dover–Dunkirk service until its closure on 22 December 1995. On 7 January 1996 she was renamed *SeaFrance Nord Pas De Calais* and following the bankruptcy of SeaFrance she entered service for My Ferry Link on 28 November 2012, on the Calais–Dover route. She left Dunkirk for Algeciras on 13 May 2016 under the name *Al Andalus Express* to be operated on the Montril–Tangier route. In 2018 she completed a two-month charter on the Las Palmas–Puerto del Rosario service.

Above left: Fiesta and Cote D'Azur.

Above right: Channel Seaway.

Below: **Fiesta,** 1980, 8,919 grt. 164x16x8m. 21 knots.
b. Kockums Varv, Malmö. Yard No. 568 IMO 7806099

    She was delivered to R/A Nordo, Malmö, as *Scandinavia* for a service from Yugoslavia to Syria. Sold to Navigation Maritime Bulgare in 1982, she was renamed *Trapezitza*, before being taken over by Sealink during an exchange between the two Seafreight ships. She was renamed *Channel Seaway* and was temporarily employed on a service from Harwich to Esbjerg and on a cargo-only Dover–Calais. Converted into a vehicle carrier with her sister by Bremer Vulkan and Lloyd Werft during 1989/90 she became *Fiesta* and was placed on the Dover–Calais cargo service. From 1990 she carried freight and passengers on the route, releasing *St Christopher*. In 1996 she became *Seafrance Cezanne* and then *Western Light* in 2011, and was beached at Alang on 16 November that year.

Dover/Folkestone–Calais/Boulogne

Above: *Anderida,* 1972, 1,601 grt. 106x16.08m. 17 knots.
b. Trosvik Verksted A/S, Kristiansund. Yard No. 95. IMO 7222229

Anderida was built for Carpass (Shipping) Company, London, on charter to British Railways' Southern Region, replacing *Shepperton Ferry*. On 1 May 1976 she was operating out of Holyhead, replacing *Preseli*, and later returned to Dover. She operated on the Heysham–Belfast route later that month after *Penda* was damaged by fire off Barrow. She also operated from Fishguard, Holyhead and Stranraer that year. On 30 October 1981 she was sold to Covenant Shipping Inc., of Monrovia, becoming *Truck Trader*. She became *Sealink* when sold to Marlborough Sealink Limited in 1985, then *Mirela* in 1986 and CTMA *Voyageur* the following year.

Below: *St Anselm,* 1980, 7,399 grt. 129x21x5m. 19½ knots.
b. Harland & Wolff, Belfast. Yard No. 1715 IMO 7813937

Designed and built for the Dover–Calais service, she operated for a short while between Fishguard and Dun Laoghaire between 28 February and 3 March 1983, resuming service at Dover on 31 March. Following an engine room fire she was repaired at Wallsend in 1990, emerging as *Stena Cambria*. The following year she was operating between Holyhead and Dun Laoghaire, becoming *Isla De Botafoc* in 1999 and then *Winner 9* in 2010. She was acquired by Ventouris Ferries and renamed *Bari* in 2010.

Above and below: *St Christopher,* 1981, 7,399 grt. 129x21x5m. 19½ knots.
b. Harland & Wolff, Belfast. Yard No. 1716 IMO 7813949

St Christopher commenced service on the Holyhead–Dun Laoghaire route and deputised for *Stena Normandica* while she was away from the Fishguard–Rosslare service in March 1981. She sailed on her maiden voyage from Dover to Calais on 15 April 1981 and following a refit at North Shields in 1991 she was renamed *Stena Antrim* to operate between Larne and Stranraer. In 1998 she was sold to Limadet, becoming IBN *Batouta*, for the Tangier–Algeciras route, and was taken over by Comanav in 2008. Following the financial collapse of her owners she was laid up at Algeciras in 2014, and was towed to Durrës in Albania by the tug *Brucoli* the following year. It is reported that she was towed to Greece in 2018.

Folkestone

Above and below: *Horsa/Stena Horsa,* 1972, 5,590 grt. 118x20x5m. 19½ knots.
b. Arsenal de Brest, Brest. Yard No. 6496/2 IMO 7205075

   Horsa entered the Folkestone–Boulogne service, releasing the *Maid of Orleans* for the Golden Arrow service. In 1984 she was the first vessel to be given the new white and blue livery and new funnel, and the following year she was grounded at Copt Point, Folkestone, in fog, damaging her propellers. She was renamed *Stena Horsa* in 1990 and took the last Boulogne sailing on 31 December 1991. Following being laid up at Milford Haven she was sold, becoming *Penelope A* for the Agoudimos Lines service between Rafina, Andros, Tinos and Mykonos. In 1999 she was sold to Minoan Flying Dolphins, being renamed *Express Penelope,* and was sold again in 2004, becoming *Penelope A*. The crew seized the vessel in 2013 due to the non-payment of wages and she was arrested the following year when she was towed from Rafina to Eleusis to be laid up.

Penelope A.

Hengist/Stena Hengist, 1972, 5,590 grt. 118x20x5m. 19½ knots.
b. Arsenal de Brest, Brest. Yard No. 6496/1 IMO 7205063

Introduced for the Folkestone–Boulogne route, she also served the Folkestone–Calais, Folkestone–Ostend and Dover–Boulogne services. On 16 October 1987 she was forced to leave her berth at Folkestone as the lines were snapping and she put to sea, where a wave caused alternator damage and she lost all electrical power. The force of the hurricane gusts drove her onto the Warren and she was finally released and towed by the tugs *Salvageman* and *Seaman* into Dover Harbour on 22 October. On 1 January 1991 she was renamed *Stena Hengist*, before becoming *Romilda* in March 1992. The following year she was acquired by Ventouris Sea Lines and was renamed *Apollo Express 2*. In 1996 she became *Panagia Ekatontapiliani*, then *Express Artemis* in 1999, *Panagia Ekatontapiliani* again in 2001 and *Agios Georgios* in 2004. She was renamed *Panagia Tinou* in 2015 and on 26 April 2016 she tilted from the right side and sank in the port of Piraeus. She was refloated and on 21 March 2017 she left Piraeus under tow for Aliaga, where she was beached two days later.

Vortigern, 1969, 4,371 grt. 114.61x19.23m. 19½ knots.
b. Swan Hunter Shipbuilding Limited, Wallsend, Newcastle. Yard No. 10 IMO 6910960

She entered service on 31 July 1969 on the Dover–Boulogne route. In June 1970 she struck and was holed by a submerged object in the Channel, and was relieved by *Maid of Kent* when she was sent to Southampton for repairs. In April 1978 she undertook a major overhaul at Smith's Dock, Middlesbrough, with an area being converted into a new 342-seat lounge. On 1 January 1979 she was transferred to Sealink UK Limited to be operated on the Folkestone–Boulogne route. At 05.24 on 4 March 1982 she was stranded across a stone groyne near Ostend due to a falling tide during a voyage from Folkestone to Ostend. She was refloated two days later and entered dry dock at Amsterdam for repairs costing over £1 million. On 2 July she collided with Folkestone Pier and was sent to Dunkirk for repairs. On 27 July 1984 she was taken over by Sea Containers Limited, Sealink British Ferries. She was arrested by the Admiralty Marshal at Portsmouth on 12 November over unpaid redundancy payments for members of the National Union of Seamen and was released the following day. On 10 January 1987 she relieved *St Brendan* at Fishguard and was chartered to Townsend-Thoresen in April for sixty days. On 1 June she was briefly laid up on the River Fal, but was swiftly brought into service again, replacing *Versailles* and *Hengist*. The following year she replaced *Stena Sailer* at Holyhead and was sold to Lindos Shipping SA of Piraeus, becoming *Milos Express* on 1 April. She was renamed *Express Milos* on 2000, *Nissos Lemnos* in 2003 and *Limon* in 2005. She was beached at Alang on 28 January 2005 and was broken up.

Newhaven

Above and below: *Falaise,* 1946, 3,710 grt. 94.64x15.1m. 20½ knots.
b. William Denny & Brothers Limited, Dumbarton. Yard No. 1400 IMO 5111969

Launched on 25 October 1946, she was delivered for the Southampton–St Malo service. She was the Southern Region's first post-war new build and could operate on any of their routes. She was transferred to the British Transport Commission on 1 January 1948. In 1964 she was converted to a car ferry and took the first dedicated car ferry sailing from Newhaven to Dieppe on 1 June. In June 1973 she operated the first drive-on/drive-off service to Jersey. The following year she suffered engine problems and was replaced by *Svea Drott*, until *Normannia* was available. On 24 December she left Holyhead in tow of the tug *Fairplay XII* for Bilbao, where she was broken up.

Senlac, 1973, 5,590 grt. 118x20x6m. 19½ knots.
b. Direction des Constructions & Armements Navales, Brest. Yard No. CF 3 IMO 7235915

Delivered to Sealink UK Limited, she commenced service between Newhaven and Dieppe on 2 May 1973. She participated in the Queen's Silver Jubilee parade on 28 June 1977. She was acquired by SNCF in January 1985, managed by Dieppe Ferries. Between 19 June and 9 September she was chartered to B&I Line for its Fishguard–Rosslare service. On 25 November 1987 she was sold to Ventouris Shipping, becoming *Apollo Express,* then *Apollo Express 1* in 1993 and *Express Apollon* in 1996. She was acquired by Minoan Flying Dolphins (Hellas Ferries) in 1999 and European Seaways in 2007. She was sold to shipbreakers and was beached at Aliaga on 1 October 2010.

For *Stena Londoner* see *Versailles* and for *Stena Parisien* see *Champs Elysées.*

Isle of Wight

Ryde, 1937, 602 grt. 66x9x4m. 14½ knots.
b. Wm Denny & Brothers, Dumbarton. Yard No. 1306 IMO 5302714

She was converted to a restaurant in 1972 and was renamed *Ryde Queen.* In 1977 she caught fire, and later became a nightclub, which closed in 1989. Since then she lay derelict and abandoned, and in 2006 her funnel collapsed. In 2018 it was announced that the PS Ryde Trust had been formed and work would commence when funding was available. However, it was later discovered that she was beyond repair and it was recommended that she should be broken up.

Brading, **1948, 837 grt. 61x15x3m. 14½ knots.**
b. Wm Denny & Brothers, Dumbarton. Yard No. 1412 IMO 5050050

She participated in the Coronation Review in 1953 and was sold to Sea Containers in 1984. She was laid up at Portsmouth in 1986, and was scrapped in 1994 by H. G. Pounds at Portsmouth.

Southsea, **1948, 837 grt. 61x15x3m. 14½ knots.**
b. Wm Denny & Brothers, Dumbarton. Yard No. 1411 IMO 5335838

In service at Portsmouth until 1986, *Southsea* was in reserve until 1997, when she was sold to Brass Patch of Lymington. Acquired by the Avon River Historic Vessel & Navigation Trust in 2001, she was broken up in 2005.

Above: *Shanklin*, 1951, 833 grt. 61x15x3m. 14½ knots.
b. Wm Denny & Brothers, Dumbarton. Yard No. 1452 IMO 5321772

In 1980 she was sold to Terry Sylvester and arrived on the Clyde on 21 November, where she was renamed *Prince Ivanhoe* by the Firth of Clyde Steam Packet Company. On 3 August 1981 she was operating a pleasure cruise starting at Penarth with calls at Minehead and Mumbles, and then a cruise along the Gower coast with 450 passengers onboard. While emerging from Port Eynon Bay she hit a submerged object, which caused an 18-metre gash in her hull, and she was beached. All of the passengers and crew were taken off by lifeboats but one passenger died from a heart attack. The hull was finally removed in July and August 1984.

Below: *Prince Ivanhoe* at Port Eynon Bay.

Above: *Fishbourne*.

Other ships include: *Camber Queen* (1961/293 grt); *Caedmon* (1973/764 grt); *Cenred* (1973/761 grt); *Cenwulf* (1973/761 grt); *Cuthred* (1969/704 grt); *St Catherine* (1983/2036 grt); *St Helen* (1983/2036 grt); *St Cecilia* (1987/2036 grt); and *St Faith* (1990/2968 grt).

South West

Weymouth–Cherbourg.

Caesarea, 1960, 4,174 grt. 98.14x16.37m. 19½ knots.
b. Samuel White & Company Limited, Cowes. Yard No. 2008 IMO 5057187

She sailed on her maiden voyage from Weymouth to the Channel Islands on 2 December 1960, and relieved on the Golden Arrow service in December/January 1966. On 11 March 1973 she was damaged by grounding at Jersey and operated her final Channel Islands sailing on 6 October 1975, prior to being transferred to Dover. In 1977 she was operating on the Folkestone–Boulogne route and was transferred to Sealink UK Limited on 1 January 1979. *Caesarea* was sold to Superluck Enterprises Incorporated in 1980, becoming *Aesarea* on arrival at Hong Kong's Shamshupo anchorage. On 9 September 1983 she was driven ashore during storm 'Ellen' but was refloated the following day. She was broken up in 1985.

Above: Cesarea.

Below: *Sarnia*, 1961, 4,174 grt. 98.14x16.37m. 19½ knots.
b. Samuel White & Company Limited, Cowes. Yard No. 2009 IMO 5314236

Sarnia was designed and built for the Channel Islands service and operated with *Caesarea* and *St Patrick*. On 28 June 1977 she was present at the Silver Jubilee Spithead Review and operated her final sailing on 10 September that year. In May 1978 she was acquired by SuperMarkets (Midland) Limited and was renamed *Aquamart*. She was laid up and left London in tow for Piraeus on 20 January 1979, where she was fitted for vehicle stern loading. Renamed *Golden Star* in 1979 and *Saudi Golden Star* in 1981, she was broken up at Gadani Beach in 1987.

Above: *Earl Godwin,* 1966, 3,999 grt. 100x18x6m. 20 knots.
b. Öresundsvarvet A/B, Landskrona. Yard No. 202 IMO 6606026

Completed as *Svea Drott* for the Stockholm–Travemunde–Copenhagen–Helsinborg service, she was chartered to replace *Falaise* when she broke down in 1974 and was renamed *Earl Godwin* the following year for the Weymouth–Channel Islands service. On 17 March 1988 she reopened a Weymouth–Cherbourg service and was chartered to P&O the following year. In 1990 she was sold to Italian interests, leaving Weymouth on 17 March as *Moby Baby*.

Below: *Svea Drott.*

Above: Earl Godwin.

Below: *Earl William*, 1964, 3,765 grt. 100x18x6m. 20 knots.
b. Öresundsvarvet A/B, Landskrona. Yard No. 160 IMO 6417047

She was delivered to Otto Thoresen A/S as car ferry *Viking II* for the Southampton–Le Havre service. Her sister *Viking I* opened the Southampton–Cherbourg route. In 1977 *Viking II* was placed on long-term charter and was renamed *Earl William* for the Portsmouth–Channel Islands service. In 1981 she replaced *Earl Granville*, and in 1984 her lease was taken over by Sea Containers Limited. In 1987 she was chartered by the United Kingdom Home Office as an immigration detention centre at Harwich. On 16/17 October she broke from her moorings and was blown ashore during a severe gale. In 1988 she operated a new Liverpool–Dun Laoghaire service. However, the service was closed the following year and she was laid up at Falmouth. She operated as relief vessel on the Holyhead and Dover–Calais services. In 1992 she was sold and renamed *Pearl William*, then *Mar Julia* in 1996, *Cesme Stern* in 1997, *Windward II* in 2000 and *Ocean Pearl* in 2006. On 2 April 2011 she was under tow by the tug *Icon 1*, which collided with a drill ship. The damage to the drill ship caused the loss of the well, which had only just started drilling. The loss was estimated to be worth around $100 million and was Lloyds' second largest loss in 2011.

Earl William laid up in the River Fal.

Above: *Earl Granville,* 1973, 4,477 grt. 109x17x5m. 19 knots.
b. Meyer, Papenburg, Ems. Yard No. 570 IMO 7310258

Built as *Viking 4* for Rederi AB Sally, Mariehamn, Finland, she was acquired by Williams & Glyn's Industrial Leasing Limited in 1980. She was renamed *Earl Granville* in August 1980 and was chartered to Sealink on a ten-year contract. In 1990 she was sold to Aegan Pelagos Naftiki Eteria of Piraeus and became *Express Olympia*. Sold to Indian shipbreakers in April 2005, she was renamed *Express O* in June and then *Mongolia* for the voyage to Alang.

Below: *Earl Granville* in the Pool of London.

Earl Harold.

Kingswear–Dartmouth

Humphrey Gilbert, 1957, 35 grt. 18x4x2m.
  b. Blackmore & Sons Limited, Bideford.

Sold to the St Mawes Ferry Company in 1977, she was later reacquired to replace the *Edith* and *Catherine* on the Tilbury–Gravesend service. *Humphrey Gilbert* and her sister *Adrian Gilbert* (1957/35 grt) were converted at Weymouth but were later refused a Board of Trade passenger certificate for service on the Thames.

Adrian Gilbert, 1957, 35 grt. 18x4x2m.
  b. Blackmore & Sons Limited, Bideford.

Fishguard

St David, 1947, 3,352 grt. 98x15x5m. 20 knots.
  b. Cammell Laird & Company Limited, Birkenhead. Yard No. 1182 IMO 530574

Transferred to the British Transport Commission in 1948, and was converted to carry cars in 1964. She was sold to Greek interests in 1971, when she was renamed *Holyhead*, and was laid up at Perama. She was broken up in 1979.

Above: *St David,* 1981, 12,619 grt. 130x21x5m. 19½ knots.
b. Harland & Wolff, Belfast Yard No. 1717 IMO 7910917

It was originally planned to operate her on the Fishguard–Rosslare route but during fitting out it was announced that she would be employed on the Holyhead–Dun Laoghaire service instead. She was transferred to the Dover–Calais route briefly in 1983 and was then moved to Holyhead, Fishguard and Stranraer–Larne. In 1990 she was renamed *Stena Caledonia* followed by *Portlink* in June 2012 for the service between Jakarta and Merak, Indonesia.

Below: *St Brendan,* 1974, 5,607 grt. 121x22x11m. 17½ knots.
b. Rickmers Rhederei GmbH, Bremerhaven. Yard No. 380 IMO 7360605

Launched for Stena A/B, Gothenburg, she was chartered to British Railways as *Stena Normandica* for the Fishguard–Rosslare route, replacing *Avalon*. In 1980 B&I Line opened a Pembroke Dock–Rosslare service with her sister, *Stena Nordica*. She was renamed *St Brendan* in 1985, *Moby Vincent* in 1989 and *Wasa Sun* in 1993 before reverting back to *Moby Vincent* the following year.

Above: Stena Normandica.

Below: **Stena Felicity**, 1980, 14,932 grt. 146x25x6m. 20 knots.
b. Öresundsvaret, Landskrona. Yard No. 278 IMO 7826788

   Delivered as *Visby* for Gotlandsbolaget, Visby, with short stroke reduction-geared diesel engines, she was chartered by Sealink for the Fishguard–Rosslare route in 1989, replacing *St Brendan*. The following year she was refitted at Falmouth, emerging as *Stena Felicity*, before becoming *Visby* in 1997, *Visborg* and *Scandinavia* in 2003 and *Rigel II* in 2015.

Holyhead

Above: *Cambria* and *Hibernia* at Holyhead.

Below: *Hibernia,* 1949, 4,973 grt. 120.7x16.52m. 21 knots.
b. Harland & Wolff Limited, Belfast. Yard No. 1367 IMO 5150111

   Hibernia arrived at Holyhead on 5 April 1949 and sailed on her maiden voyage to Dun Laoghaire on 14 April. In 1951 she had Denny Brown stabilisers fitted and she was modernised during her winter overhaul in 1964. In December 1967 she operated on the Heysham–Belfast route and was transferred to a Heysham–Dun Laoghaire route following the fire at Menai Bridge in May 1971. Her final sailing from Holyhead to Dun Laoghaire took place on 2/3 October 1975. On 5 October 1975 she was laid up at Barrow. She sailed to Piraeus following her sale to Agipatos Brothers on 1 December 1976, and was renamed *Express Apollon*. She was laid up on 15 December 1976 and arrived at Bombay to be broken up on 18 December 1980. She then sailed to Darukhana, India, on 12 January 1981 and was broken up by Solid Steel Traders.

Above: *Cambria*, 1949, 4,973 grt. 120.7x16.52m. 21 knots.
b. Harland & Wolff Limited, Belfast. Yard No. 1368 IMO 5059020

Delivered for the Holyhead–Dun Laoghaire service, during her 1951 overhaul she was fitted with Denny Brown stabilisers. On 15 June 1953 she was present at the Coronation Review at Spithead. It was originally intended to send *Amsterdam* but she was retained in service due to a collision involving *Duke of York*. In 1971 *Cambria* and *Hibernia* operated from Heysham following a fire on the Britannia Bridge, which connects Anglesey with mainland Wales. She was sold to Orri Navigation Lines, Jeddah, in 1976, becoming *Al Taif*. On 15 January 1981 she sank while at anchor in Suez Roads.

Below: *Stena Hibernia*, 1977, 7,836 grt. 129.2x21.2m.
b. Aalborg Vaerft, Aalborg. Yard No. 214 IMO 7507019

She was launched on 17 July 1976 as *St Columba* for the Holyhead–Dun Laoghaire service. In 1991 she became *Stena Hibernia*, then *Stena Adventurer* in 1996, *Express Afroditi* in 1997 and *Masarrah* in 2007.

Above: St Columba.

Below: St Columba.

Above: Express Afroditi.

Below: Masarrah.

Above: *Stena Cambria*.

Below: *St Cybi*, 1975, 2,353 grt. 119x16x11m. 18 knots.
b. Verolme Cork Dockyards, Cork. Yard No. 22/874 IMO 7365069

Delivered as *Dundalk* for the B&I Line, she was renamed *Stena Sailer* in 1980. In 1982 she was chartered to Sealink for the Harwich–Hook of Holland route, followed by a charter to North Sea Ferries and the Isle of Man Steam Packet Company in 1983. The following year she operated between Belfast and Heysham for Belfast Freight Ferries and was later laid up at Falmouth. In 1987 she operated between Holyhead and Dun Laoghaire, and Fishguard and Rosslare, becoming *St Cybi* the following year. In 1991 she was renamed *Wind Cybi* and then became *Theseus* in 1992. On 29 May 2006 she arrived at Aliaga and was broken up.

Holyhead–Belfast/Dublin

Slieve Bearnagh, 1936, 1,450 grt. 91x14x5m.
b. William Denny & Brothers Limited, Dumbarton. Yard No. 1293 IMO 5332020
Converted to oil burning in 1961, she was sold to Spanish shipbreakers at Gijon ten years later.

Slieve Bawn, 1936, 1,447 grt. 94x14x5m. 16½ knots.
b. William Denny & Brothers Limited, Dumbarton. Yard No. 1299 IMO 5332018
Converted to oil burning in 1961, she was sold to Spanish shipbreakers at Gijon in 1972.

Slieve Donard, 1960, 1,598 grt. 95x14x5m. 13½ knots.
B. Ailsa Ship Building Company, Troon. Yard No. 506 IMO 5332044
Converted at Birkenhead for the carriage of sheep in 1976, she left the Mersey as *Arabi* for Jeddah. She was broken up at Gadani Beach in 1987.

Brian Boroime, 1970, 4,098grt. 107x17x8m. 14 knots.
b. Verolme Cork Dockyards, Cork. Yard No. 11/809 IMO 7015327
She was delivered for the Holyhead–Dublin and Holyhead–Belfast routes. In 1989 she was laid up at Falmouth and was sold the following year, becoming *Peltainer,* and then *Abdul H* in 2004. She was broken up at Aliaga in 2012.

Rhodi Mawr, 1970, 4,098 grt. 107x17x8m. 14 knots.
b. Verolme Cork Dockyards, Cork. Yard No. 12/810 IMO 7019220
Sister to *Brian Boroime*, she was employed on the Heysham–Belfast service in 1970 following the fire on the Britannia Bridge, Anglesey. Transferred to Holyhead in 1972, she completed a short period at Harwich with *Brathay Fisher* in 1978. She was sold in 1990 and renamed *Peliner*, then *Destiny* in 2004 and *Yamm* in 2010. She arrived at Aliaga on 17 November 2014 and was broken up.

Heysham

Duke of Argyll, 1956, 4,797 grt. 114.63x17.46m. 21 knots.
b. Harland & Wolff Limited, Belfast. Yard No. 1541 IMO 5094460

She was converted into a stern-loading car ferry by her builders in 1969–70 and made her final Heysham–Belfast sailing on 6 April 1975. Sold later that year, she was renamed *Neptunia* for service in Greece. In 1984 she operated as a Schools Abroad ship and became *Corinthia* in 1988, followed by *Faith Power* in 1994, then *Fairy Princess* and *Zenith* in 1995. She suffered a serious engine room fire in 1995 and was run aground, before being refloated and sold for scrap.

Neptunia.

Above: Duke of Lancaster, 1956, 4,797 grt. 114.63x17.46m. 21 knots.
b. Harland & Wolff Limited, Belfast. Yard No. 1540 IMO 5094496

She was launched on 14 December 1955 for the Heysham–Belfast service. In 1966 she operated three and four-day cruises and in 1969 she was converted to a stern loading car ferry. On 6 April 1975 the Heysham–Belfast service discontinued and she operated on the Fishguard–Rosslare route, and then the Holyhead–Dun Laoghaire in 1975. Her final sailing from Holyhead to Dun Laoghaire took place on 9 November 1978, and she was laid up at Holyhead. She was transferred to Sealink UK Limited on 1 January 1979. She was then laid up at Barrow and was sold to Empirewise Limited. She was towed to Mostyn in August 1979 and was renamed *Duke of Llanerch-y-Mor*. In May 1980 she opened as a leisure facility without planning permission. The owners have been in dispute with the local council ever since, but the ship has remained closed. The coin-operated arcade machines were sold in 2012 and there are now plans to transform the hull into the largest open-air gallery in the United Kingdom.

Below: *Duke of Lancaster* at Belfast.

Duke of Lancaster in North Wales.

Duke of Rothesay, 1956, 4,797 grt. 114.63x17.46m. 21 knots.
b. Wm Denny & Brothers, Dumbarton. Yard No. 1487 IMO 5094513

She was converted to a side-loader in 1967 and was employed on the Fishguard–Rosslare service. In 1974 she was used on the Dover–Calais route, replacing *Maid of Orleans*, and arrived at Shipbreaking Industries, Faslane, on 18 October 1975 to be broken up.

Duke of Rothesay on the Heysham–Belfast service.

Container Enterprise, 1958, 982 grt. 81x13x5m. 10 knots.
   b. Ailsa Ship Building Company, Troon. Yard No. 500 IMO 5079018

Container Venturer, 1958, 982 grt. 81x13x5m. 10 knots.
   b. Ailsa Ship Building Company, Troon. Yard No. 501 IMO 5079020

Manx Viking, 1976, 2,753grt 102x17x11m. 18 knots.
b. S. A. Juliana Constructora Gijonesa, Gijon. Yard No. 243 IMO 7387251

   Launched as *Monte Cruceta*, she was delivered as *Monte Castillo* for Naviera Aznar SA, Bilbao. She was acquired by Manx Line Limited in 1978 for the Heysham–Douglas service. In 1987 she was sold to Det Stavangerske Dampskibsselskab, becoming *Manx*, then *Skudenes*, *Ontario No. 1* and *Nindawayma* in 1989.

Ontario No. 1.

Lake District
Tern, 1891, 120 grt. 43x6x2m.
    b. Forrest & Company, Wivenhoe, Essex.

Swift, 1900, 203 grt. 46x6x3m.
    b. T. B. Seath & Company, Rutherglen.

Teal, 1936, 251 grt. 41x8x2m.
b. Vickers Armstrong Limited, Barrow.

Swan, 1936, 251 grt. 41x8x2m.
  b. Vickers Armstrong Limited, Barrow. Managed by Sealink UK Limited.

Gondola, 1859, 42 grt.
  b. Jones, Quiggin Limited, Liverpool.

Stranraer–Larne

Larne–Stranraer.

Caledonian Princess, 1961, 3,630 grt. 107.59x16.76m. 20½ knots.
b. William Denny & Brothers Limited, Dumbarton. Yard No. 1501 IMO 5057840

Launched on 5 April 1961, she was delivered for the Stranraer–Larne service on 24 November. She sailed on her maiden voyage on 16 December, and on 6 July 1964 she was joined by *Slieve Donard*, which was able to carry sixty cars. In 1965 *Lohengrin* was chartered to operate alongside *Caledonian Princess*; in 1966 *Stena Nordica* was also chartered to assist *Caledonian Princess* on the route. On 1 January 1967 she was transferred to the British Railways Board and on 28 May 1968 she was moved to the Holyhead–Dun Laoghaire route, to operate with *Holyhead Ferry 1*. On 1 January 1969 she was owned by British Transport Ship Management (Scotland) Limited. Side-loader doors were fitted and she was transferred to the Fishguard–Rosslare summer service. She returned to the Stranraer–Larne route in May 1970, operating with *Baltic Ferry* and later *Stena Trailer*. Between 11 May and 21 June 1972 she operated on the Newhaven–Dieppe service and replaced *Duke of Rothesay* on the Fishguard–Rosslare route on 27 June 1972, before later returning to the Stranraer–Larne service. On 28 June 1973 she was joined by *Neckartal* and in 1975 she became the standby vessel at Newhaven, later operating on the Weymouth–Channel Islands route. In 1981 she was refitted and then based at Dover. Laid up at Newhaven on 11 October 1981, she was sold to the Michael Quadrini Group on 14 December 1982. On 27 February 1983 she was towed to Gateshead and was renamed *Tuxedo Princess* while owned by Riverzest Limited. In July 1988 she arrived at Glasgow under tow, as *Caledonian Princess*. In 1998 she was moved back to the River Tyne and moored at Gateshead, becoming *Tuxedo Princess* again. In 2008 she was renamed *Prince* and arrived at Aliaga on 23 August 2008 to be broken up.

Above: *Caledonian Princess* at Dun Laoghaire

Below: *Caledonian Princess* at sea.

Above: *Caledonian Princess* postcard.

Below: *Caledonian Princess* on the River Tyne.

Above: *Antrim Princess,* 1967, 3,270 grt. 112.65x17.4m. 19½ knots.
b. Hawthorn Leslie (Shipbuilders) Limited, Hebburn. Yard No. 765 IMO 6714562

Launched on 24 April 1967, she sailed on her maiden voyage on 17 December from Stranraer to Larne. On 1 January 1969 she was transferred to British Transport Ship Management (Scotland) Limited and in 1980 she carried out relief duties on the English Channel. On 16 October 1980 she operated on the Douglas–Heysham route and on 9 December 1983 she suffered a serious engine room fire and was disabled. It was decided to take her 108 passengers and her thirty-one crew off by RAF helicopter. The tug HMS *Rolliker* arrived as the power was restored. She was towed into Belfast for repairs on 10 December and returned to service on 28 December. In 1985 she was on charter to the Isle of Man Steam Packet Company for the Heysham–Douglas service and was renamed *Tynwald* in 1986. Her final sailing on the Heysham–Douglas route was on 18 February 1990 and she was laid up on the River Fal on 22 February. In March 1990 she was sold to Agostino Lauro s.r.l., and was renamed *Lauro Express*. She became *Giuseppe D'Abundo* in 2003 and then *Stella* in 2006. She arrived at Alang on 19 January 2007 and was broken up.

Below: *Antrim Princess* at Larne.

Above: *Antrim Princess* at Douglas.

Below: *Antrim Princess* becomes *Tynwald* at Birkenhead.

Above: *Ailsa Princess,* 1971, 6,177 grt. 113x17x4m. 20 knots.
b. Ansaldo & Company, Genoa at Cantieri Navale, Venice. Yard No. 272 IMO 7038379

Delivered for service on the Stranraer–Larne route, in 1975 she operated for a short time between Ardrossan and Larne. In 1982 she was chartered to the Ministry of Defence and was rebuilt at Birkenhead, reverting back to a car ferry in January the following year. Renamed *Earl Harold* in 1985, and in 1989 she was chartered to the B&I Line for the Pembroke Dock–Rosslare service. Later that year she became *Dimitra*, followed by *Naias Express* in 1994, *Express Adonis* in 2000 and *New Caribbean Princess* in 2006. She was acquired by Samudra Link Shipping in 2006, becoming *New Cambay Prince,* and was broken up in India in 2010.

Below: Naias Express.

Darnia, 1977, 2,807 grt. 114x18x11m. 18 knots.
   b. Österreichische Schiffwerften AG, Linz-Korneuburg. Yard No. 710 IMO 7501297
   She became *Nord Neptunus* in 1991 and *Neptunia* in 1997, and was broken up at Aliaga in 2007.

Ulidia, 1971, 1,600 grt. 106x16x11m. 17 knots.
b. Kristiansands M/V, A/S, Kristiansand. Yard No. 215 IMO 7033202
   She was renamed *Auto Trader* in 1981, *Raga Queen* in 1986, *Fjordveien* in 1988, *Fjardvagen* in 1994, *Holger Stjern* in 1995, *Holger* in 1999, *Meltem G* in 2005 and *Lider Avrasya* in 2009. She was broken up in 2011.

Dalriada, 1971, 1,600 grt. 106x16x11m. 17 knots.
   b. Brodrene Lothe A/S, Haugesund. Yard No. 31 IMO 7105081
   Launched as *Stena Trailer,* she became *Viking Trader* in 1980, *Stena Trader* in 1981, *Trader* and *Trailer* in 1985, *Sarmacja* in 1991, *Wolin* in 1992, *Mesuji* in 1993 and *Lampung* in 1994. She was lost in 2006.

Stena Antrim.

Stena Caledonia.

Galloway Princess/Stena Galloway, 1980, 6,506 grt. 129x22x12m. 18½ knots.
b. Harland & Wolff & Company Limited, Belfast. Yard No. 1713 IMO 7719430

Launched for Sealink UK Limited, she was owned by Midland Montague Leasing Limited and passed into the ownership of Sea Containers Limited in 1984. She became *Stena Galloway* in 1991 and *Le Rif* in 2002.

Le Rif.

Humber

Tattershall Castle, 1934, 556 grt. 61x10x3m.
b. Wm Gray & Company, West Hartlepool. Yard No. 1059 IMO 5353804

She was berthed at London's Victoria Embankment, having had arrived on the Thames in 2011, and operated as a floating restaurant.

Wingfield Castle, 1934, 550 grt. 61x10x3m.
b. Wm Gray & Company, West Hartlepool. Yard No. 1060 IMO 5392018

Following withdrawal from service, it was intended to use her as a floating restaurant in Swansea Marina, but she was too wide to fit through the lock gates. She is now preserved at the Museum of Hartlepool as a floating exhibit.

Lincoln Castle, 1940, 598 grt. 61x10x3m.
b. A&J Inglis Limited, Pointhouse. Yard No. 1024 IMO 5208671

She was the last coal-fired paddle steamer in regular service in the United Kingdom and served as a restaurant at Hessle and later at Alexandra Dock, Grimsby. She was broken up in October 2010.

| Length | 153.1m | Cars | 240 | G.R.T. | 12,343 | Service speed | 22 knots |
| Breadth | 22.0m | Cabins | 329 | N.R.T. | 6,198 | Passengers | 650 |

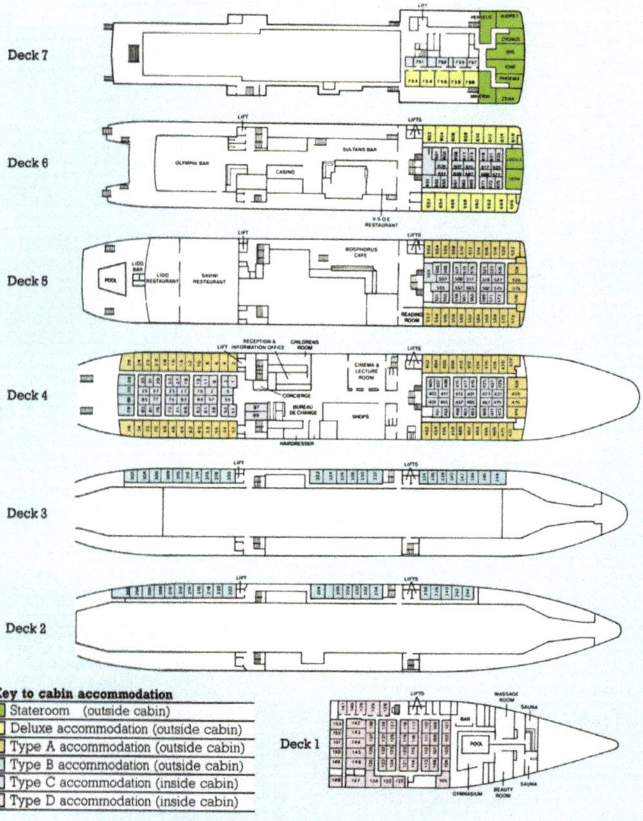

Key to cabin accommodation
- Stateroom (outside cabin)
- Deluxe accommodation (outside cabin)
- Type A accommodation (outside cabin)
- Type B accommodation (outside cabin)
- Type C accommodation (inside cabin)
- Type D accommodation (inside cabin)

92

Opposite page and right: *Orient Express*, 1975, 16,546 grt.
b. Dubigeon-Normandie, Prairie au Duc. Yard No. 143 IMO 7360198

She was built as *Bore Star*, becoming *Orient Express* in 1980, *Silja Star* and *Club Sea* in 1986, *Eurosun* in 1989, *Orient Sun* in 1991, *Wasa Queen* in 2001, *Alberta* in 2009 and *Amet Majesty* in 2011.

Meeching, 1960, 152 grt. 30x8x4m. 12½ knots.
b. P. K. Harris & Son Limited, Appledore. Yard No. 127 IMO 5230686

A tug based at Dover.

Landguard, 1960, 674 grt. 48x11m.
b. Goole Shipbuilding Company. Yard No. 520 IMO 5203140
Based at Fishguard as a pilot transfer boat.

Workboats

Pinmill at Harwich.
Nic at Guernsey.
Joanne and *Alice II* at Portsmouth.
Melcombe I, *Melcombe II* and *Melcombe III* at Weymouth.
Triton and *Charon* at Holyhead.

Charters

Armorique
1986, prior to delivery of
Koningin Beatrix.
Harwich–Hook of Holland.

Auersberg
July/August 1992.
Holyhead–Dun Laoghaire.

Baltic Ferry
1971.
Stranraer–Larne.

Breizh-Izel
1982, while *Darnia* was having additional accommodation fitted.
Stranraer–Larne.

C R Casablanca
1989, to provide additional tonnage on the route.
Dieppe–Newhaven.

Carsten
1971, following the grounding of *Selby*.
Channel Islands service.

Celebrity
1979, following loss of Douglas linkspan.
Douglas–Heysham.

Cerdic Ferry
1978.
Stranraer–Larne.

Clyde
Tilbury–Gravesend.

Colchester
1969–75.
Harwich–Rotterdam.

Cornouailles
1984–86.
Dieppe–Newhaven.

Dana Anglia
1987.
Harwich–Hook of Holland.

Darlington
1969–71.
Southampton–Channel Islands.
Heysham–Dublin.

Domburgh
1969–73.
Harwich–Rotterdam.

Donautal/Ulster Sportsman
1971–75.
Heysham–Belfast.

Duchesse Anne
1989.
Harwich–Hook of Holland.

Eden Fisher
1966–68.
Fishguard–Waterford.
1979, Douglas–Heysham.

Elk
1969–72.
Weymouth–Channel Islands.

Firth Fisher
Heysham–Belfast.

Flamborian
February/March 1972.
Hull–New Holland.

Free Enterprise II
1980/1981.
Weymouth–Channel Islands.
Dieppe–Newhaven.

Free Enterprise III
Summer 1981, following *Caledonian Princess*'s transfer to the Channel Islands route.
Dover–Calais/Boulogne.

Gotland
1988.
Dieppe–Newhaven.

Guernsey Fisher
1971–77.
Portsmouth–Channel Islands.

Harrogate
1969–72.
Fishguard–Waterford.
Heysham/Holyhead–Dublin.

Hera
1994–95.
Harwich–Zeebrugge.

Highland Seabird
1980.
Portsmouth–Ryde.
1982, Tilbury–Gravesend.

Island Scene
1989.
Portsmouth–Ryde.

Isle of Ely
1969–76.
Weymouth–Channel Islands.

Jenny M
1989.
Portsmouth–Ryde.

Jersey Fisher
1972–77.
Portsmouth–Channel Islands.

Jetferry One
1981, cover for damaged *Princesse Clementine*.
Ostend–Dover.

Kingsnorth Fisher
1971.
To rescue locomotives stranded at Anglesey, following the fire on the Britannia Bridge.

Lady of Mann
1990.
Holyhead–Dun-Laoghaire.

Lagan Bridge
1979–80.
Heysham–Belfast.

Lune Bridge
1979–80.
Heysham–Belfast.
Portsmouth–Channel Islands.

Lune Fisher
1969–72.
Southampton–Channel Islands.

Marine Evangeline
1986–87.
1995.
Dieppe–Newhaven.

Mercandian Universe
1989.
Harwich services.

Mona's Queen
1989.
Portsmouth–Cherbourg.

Mouse
1969–72.
Weymouth–Channel Islands.

Nassau
1972–73.
Harwich–Rotterdam.

Neckartal
1974–77.
Fishguard–Rosslare.
Larne–Stranraer.

Nora Heeren
1994–95.
Harwich–Zeebrugge.

Norrona
1994/1995.
Holyhead–Dun Laoghaire.
Fishguard–Rosslare.

Penda
1975–80.
Heysham–Belfast.

Penn-ar-Bed
1982.
Felixstowe–Dunkerque.

Pool Fisher
1979.
Douglas–Heysham.

Preseli
1974–77.
Fishguard–Rosslare.
Heysham–Belfast.

Prinsessan Desiree
1981.
Holyhead–Dun Laoghaire.

Prinz Oberon
1983.
Harwich–Hook of Holland.

RoRo Cimbria
1978.
Dieppe–Newhaven.

RoRo Dania
1975.
Stranraer–Larne.

Ryde Rapide
1983.
Portsmouth–Ryde.

Saaletal
1971–73.
Heysham–Belfast.

Sailormark
1973.
Heysham–Belfast.

Saint Patrick II
1989, Portsmouth–Cherbourg.
1989/90, Dover–Calais.

Scandinavica
1988.
Dover–Calais/Zeebrugge

Selby
1969–73.
Heysham–Dublin/Belfast.

Skarvoy
1989.
Portsmouth–Channel Islands.

Solent Enterprise
1980.
1989.
Portsmouth–Ryde.

Solent Scene
1989.
Portsmouth–Ryde.

Stena Nordica
1966–71.
Stranraer–Larne.

Stena Sea Lynx
1993–95.
Holyhead–Dun Laoghaire.
Fishguard–Rosslare.

Stena Sea Lynx II
1994–95.
Holyhead–Dun Laoghaire.

Stena Timer
1979–80.
Stranraer–Larne.
Holyhead–Dun Laoghaire.

Stena Traveller
1992.
Harwich–Hook of Holland.
Southampton–Cherbourg.

Thjelvar
Portsmouth–Cherbourg.

Transbaltica
1978.
Holyhead–Dun Laoghaire.

Vanquisher
Tilbury–Gravesend.

Viking Victory
1978, Channel Islands.
1981, Douglas–Heysham.

Viking III
1981.
Douglas–Heysham.

Vinzia E
1993.
Newhaven–Dieppe.

Winchester
1969–71.
Jersey/St Malo routes.

Yorkshire Belle
Occasional cover in the
1960s/1970s.
Hull–New Holland.

Zeeland
1984–86.
Harwich–Hook of Holland.

Managed by Sealink UK Limited

Gondola, 1859, 42 grt
b. Jones, Quiggin Limited,
Liverpool.
Coniston–Park a Moor.